D0898409

# HALAL MONK

## *A Christian on a Journey through Islam*

Jonas Yunus Atlas

**HALAL MONK**
A CHRISTIAN ON A JOURNEY THROUGH ISLAM.
Jonas Yunus Atlas

\*

*www.halalmonk.com*
*www.jonasyunus.net*

\*

Yunus Publishing
2014

ISBN 978-9-08-149964-4

\*

© Yunus Publishing

*Nothing in this work can be multiplied and/or made public by any means of print, photocopy, microfilm, digital documents or in any other way without the written authorisation of the author.*

# TABLE OF CONTENTS

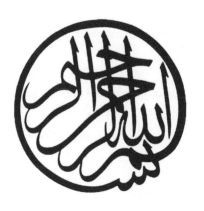

# INTRODUCTION

# ABOUT THE CLASH
# OF CIVILISATIONS

The idea that we are witnessing a clash of civilisations has strongly taken root all over the world. It has convinced many people that the Islamic world and the West are inherently opposed. The West is, therefore, often portrayed as the pinnacle of a just democracy, built on the values of the enlightenment, in stark contrast to the image of a despotic Islamic world, built on the premises of the Qur'an. Throughout mainstream media, this dichotomy is frequently repeated in various ways. On one side you can see the freedom loving Westerner, on the other side a bearded fundamentalist who's ready to bomb everyone that stands in the way of a theocracy.

The spread of this imagery obviously has a lot to do with what happened that one day on the 11th of September in 2001. We should not forget, however, that the discourse on the clash of civilisations had actually risen to the forefront many years before that tragic event. Many socio-political analysts have pointed out how we can easily trace the origins of the current opposition between the Western and the Islamic worlds to the time when the social scare of communism had gradually fallen away. In other words, the concept of clashing civilisations wasn't a sudden academic discovery. Rather, it was a sociological hunch, which steadily filled the void that originated after the previous 'us versus them' story of the Cold War had disappeared. It is quite symbolic in this respect that the year 1989 did not only witness the fall of the Berlin Wall, but also brought us the controversy around the fatwa of Ayatollah Ruhollah Khomeini, which legitimized the killing of Salman Rushdie, the author of the novel, *The Satanic Verses*.

Hence, in spite of what many people might think, today's ideology of cultural confrontation wasn't born out of the shock of 9/11 and its aftermath. What happened that day was merely a catalyst. The whole idea had more than a decade of incubation time before it truly erupted and engulfed us all at an enormous speed.

---

Some people had seen it coming,[1] but the rapid spread of this new ideology took many people by surprise. I only became truly aware of it myself in 2006 while living in Istanbul for a year. It was only because I coincidentally lived on 'the other side' that I started to sense the magnitude of the ever growing fear of Islam. And it left me utterly puzzled.

As a Christian theologian, I had always been very interested in different religions. Ever since my adolescence I had deepened my knowledge of Buddhist and Hindu traditions, which had a strong influence on my personal Christian convictions and spiritual practice. Initially, therefore, I didn't really focus on Islam. I most certainly looked upon Islam as one of the many great religious traditions of our world and I was convinced it could be a genuine source of inspiration for my own Christian views on the world and the divine. Yet, because of simple coincidence, I had not acquainted myself with this religion before my late twenties. That drastically changed, of course, when I resided in Turkey, where my

---

[1] Dr. D. Latifa and Ziauddin Sardar, for example, who appear later in this book, wrote articles and essays about these evolutions long before the events of 9/11.

fascination grew day by day.

During that same period, however, Islam seemed to turn into the world's utmost bogeyman as well. The open-ended 'war on Islamic terrorism'[2] had been installed and doubts were raised about the presence of Islam in Western societies.

Gradually, I felt ever more disconnected from my own European society. Its growing fear of this particular religious tradition shocked me. I noticed how people did not only fear Muslims in countries which they knew little about, but also became scared of the possible radicalization of Muslims in their own neighbourhoods. The distrust grew palpably; gradually, many questions were raised whether Muslims in Western communities can in fact be Muslim *and* democratic at the same time, whether they can follow Islam *and* support Western values.

Nowadays, ever more people are convinced that those questions have to be answered in the negative and, as such, Muslims have once again become the fearful and dark enemy.

I say 'once again' because ever since the arrival of the Muslim community on the geo-political scene of history, this friction has often surfaced. The Crusades are probably the most radical example thereof. And, quite startlingly, President Bush actually used the word 'crusade' to legitimize the military actions that were to be taken in the aftermath of 9/11.

To make matters even worse, I could (and can) also easily see that a similar fear of the other was (and is) growing just as rapidly in many parts of the Muslim world – though, of course, the other way around. Many political and religious leaders of the Muslim community increasingly seem to deny the possibility of harmony and succeed in propagating ever more rigid interpretations of

---

2 I use the phrase 'war on Islamic terrorism' and not 'war on terror' since this 'war' only legitimized military actions in Islamic countries. The rhetoric was never used to fight against separatist terrorism in Europe, for example, even though, in Europe, separatist terrorism has made a lot more victims than religiously inspired terrorism in the last decade.

Islam.

———— ❂ ————

The Crusades obviously were an undeniable black page in the history of the Catholic Church and can easily be seen as a negation of Christ's teachings. Quite the contrary, my own faith in Christ's example has always inspired me to approach any potential conflict with a sincere search for soul.

In my own small way, then, I wished to go deeper. I wanted to acquaint myself with the soul of Islam. I wanted to try to take some steps beyond the conflict. That's how the Halal Monk was born.

# ABOUT THE HALAL MONK

The Halal Monk is a Christian on a journey through Islam.

I'm not an ordained monk, however, nor am I connected to a specific monastic order. With the title of this book, and the project that preceded it, I above all wished to combine elements of both the Islamic and the Christian traditions. It also invokes a modern adaptation of the times when religious figures would travel around to discuss theology and spirituality with people of different faiths, for that's what I started doing. By combining my academic background in philosophy, anthropology and theology with my experience in activism, blogging and writing, I brought about a series of fascinating conversations with influential people of the Muslim world. I met with important spiritual leaders and artists to engage in a dialogue about several topics on the intersection of culture, society and religion.

These conversations were gathered on the project's website, www.halalmonk.com. Some of them found their way to different news sites and Dutch translations were published on community sites in the Netherlands and Belgium. As such, they gradually reached a wider audience and stirred some debate.

———— ❄ ————

Within efforts of interreligious dialogue, the more difficult questions are often circumvented by superficial talks in which the different parties respectfully listen but seldom truly engage. I wanted to go further. I wanted to have more in-depth conversations, for within that depth I hoped to find unexpected solutions for the cultural problems we are now facing on a global scale.

Because my journey as the Halal Monk is quite personal, however, I did not try to be as 'representative' as possible in my choice of the people I talked to. I had two very simple criteria. They had to have a certain amount of international influence and I needed to be intrigued by their specific teachings, art or expertise.

Perhaps, then, some people might regret that I didn't have any conversations with spiritual leaders from Africa or artists from the Arabian Peninsula. Others might think that I should have focussed on a wider variety of spiritual strands or intellectual positions. And still others might miss specific names that are of huge importance in certain regions of the Islamic world.

Nevertheless, one will find a balance of women and men, of people who were born as Muslims and converts, of more conservative and very progressive voices from all layers and corners of the Muslim world. Throughout my journey, I have met with important scholars, musicians, imams, academics, activists, photographers, fashion designers, stand-up artists and journalists from the United States, Indonesia, the United Kingdom, Pakistan, Turkey, The Netherlands, Egypt, Morocco, Belgium, France, Mali, Germany, Malaysia and Canada.

Thus, over the years, I have developed an intimate bond with the Muslim world. The various conversations have greatly inspired me and brought me new insights. Yet, I have never considered leaving my own Christian tradition behind. If anything, my many encounters seemed to strengthen my faith. Not because they made me more convinced of certain truths, but because they amplified my love for the Divine.

# ABOUT THIS BOOK

As the Halal Monk, I have travelled quite far and, thus, it became time to write down some sort of 'travelogue'. Therefore, in this book, I share those conversations which I deemed most important, innovative and beautiful so that they might be read as a whole.

Some conversations, however, that are dear to my heart sadly did not make it into the book. Some examples are a discussion on Islamic finance with Ajaz Ahmed Khan, a talk with Ousmane Ag Moussa about the struggle of the Tuareg, as well as a conversation with U-Cef, an artist who creates a fusion of Moroccan Gnawa music with electronic beats and who, in fact, once made a song called 'Halal Monk' (and kindly allowed me to take up that same title). The conversations that aren't included in this book can, of course, always be found on halalmonk.com.

Yet, to maintain a proper flow, limitations simply had to be made somewhere. I had to stick to the most 'essential' topics in this book and I left out certain themes that are a bit more 'on the side'.

On the other hand, this book isn't meant as an introductory text. It explicitly tries to go beyond the basics and the typical discussions.

Perhaps, then, the reader of this book should already have some knowledge of Islam in order to grasp everything that is discussed in the various conversations. Nevertheless, even if the reader does not have much knowledge of Islam, the whole should still be accessible since the book attempts to gradually take the reader deeper into 'the unknown'.

Furthermore, particular aspects of Islamic theology, history and society are progressively explained in a very organic way. As such, this book actually goes back and forth between the basics and beyond. In the present day discussions on Islam, the basics simply do not suffice. Yet, as any sincere spiritual wayfarer knows, to go beyond the basics, one also constantly has to return to those basics.

It is, in fact, the constant motion between basics and beyond that can free us from stereotypes – not only from stereotypes of conflict, but also from stereotypes of toothpaste smiles that oh so happily shout 'yay for common ground!' For the only true unity is the one that allows diversity.

———— ❁ ————

I, thus, hope this book can serve two purposes. First of all, it should be able to inspire Muslims because of the sometimes less heard ideas which are put forth by many of the scholars and artists I spoke to. At the same time, it should offer Christians the possibility of gaining a better understanding of Islam – in its similarities as well as its differences.

Because of the twofold purpose of this book, every conversation is also preceded by a short description of an Islamic term. As the reader will notice, these descriptions are addressed to Christians. After all, the book is the reflection of a journey of a Christian through Islam. These explanations of theological and spiritual concepts will, therefore, not only offer some necessary background to the reader who doesn't have any roots in the Islamic tradition, but will also serve as the spiritual glue between the different conversations and, in a way, reveal the underlying journey. As such, they aren't typical encyclopaedic expositions either. One could just open a dictionary or go to Wikipedia to look up some dry definitions of terms. However, in line with the purpose of this book, I tried to create 'bridging explanations'. That is to say, the Islamic concepts are compared to spiritual aspects of Christianity and they are placed within the contemporary socio-political context.[3]

The specific choice of concepts isn't encyclopaedic either. I didn't decide to discuss these terms and theological tenets because of their supposed ideological importance in the framework of the Islamic religion. Rather, I chose them because of their spiritual importance, because of their presence in the conversations or because of the tension that surrounds them in the present day global debates.

It would make little sense to only portray certain beautiful aspects of the history, theology and spirituality of Islam and leave out exactly those things that seem to cause so much friction. True dialogue dares to confront. As such, the often problematic topics are actually the starting point of many of the conversations that are contained in this book.

Yet, if true dialogue dares to confront, it does not only confront 'the other'. The true nature of sincere dialogue above all lies in the courage to confront the self.

---

[3] In line with all of this, Arabic or lesser known words of the Islamic tradition are placed in italics when mentioned for the first time. They will be explained by a footnote, unless the text itself elaborates on their meaning. These words are also collected in the glossary at the back of the book for quick reference.

# Acknowledgements

My sincere thanks go to the teams behind the Dutch website, nieuwemoskee.nl, and the Belgian website, kifkif.be, for their continued support and the manner in which they helped to give a wider audience to the Halal Monk conversations.

I would also like to express my sincere appreciation to the different photographers who kindly allowed me to use their pictures in this book and on the cover. In this respect, I would especially like to thank Mark Kohn, Irna Qureshi, Redouan Tijani, Mohammed Anwerzada, Enid Bloch and Sophie Slaats.

Finally, my deepest gratitude goes to Ali Shirazi and his wife, Nida e Zainab, for their help in organizing the meeting with Abida Parveen, as well as their patience during the transcription process of my conversations with Abida Parveen and Muazzam Fateh Ali Khan. About half a year after Ali and Nida helped me with those transcriptions, Ali's father and brother were murdered by militant extremists. They were on their way to the Friday prayer during the month of Ramadan when they were shot because of their specific spiritual convictions. In a bitter and painful way, it made the conversations in this book even more relevant. It seems only natural, therefore, to dedicate this book to Ali, Nida and their family.

و السلام عليكم ورحمة الله وبركاته

*Photograph Abdulwahid Van Bommel © Mark Kohn*
*Photograph Aki Nawaz © Irna Qureshi*
*Photograph Amir Sulaiman © Redouan Tijani*
*Photograph accompanying the conversation with*
*Dr. D. Latifa © Mohammed Anwerzada*
*Photograph Cyrus McGoldrick © Ariane Moshayedi*
*Photograph Feisal Abdul Rauf © Enid Bloch*
*Photograph Kudsi Ergüner © Wijnand Schouten*
*Photograph Peter Sanders © John Gulliver*
*Photograph Abida Parveen (creative commons) Torre Urnes*
*Photograph Jonas Yunus on the back cover © Sophie Slaats*
*Photograph Badshahi mosque © Haider Azim/Fotolia*

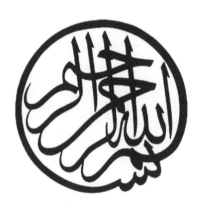

# ON THE CROSSROADS
# OF TRADITION AND
# MODERNITY

# ISLAM

The literal translation of the word 'Islam' is 'submission'. It refers to the humbleness of a soul that immerses itself within the divine flow of life. Critics often remove this spiritual aspect from the word and literalize the idea of 'submission' to an obligation of mindlessly following specific rules and regulations. To them, the very name of the religion is yet another example of how Islam, in general, is a rigid and uncompromising faith that does not allow any freedom or dissent.

Such critics see the Islamic world as a homogenous block, totally stuck within primitive ideas and suffocating social patterns. Sadly enough, their view has been taken up by a great number of people.

Yet, even though it is undeniable that in many places dissention is easily dismissed or destroyed, on a more global level, Muslims find themselves in the middle of innovating debates. An enormous amount of theological, philosophical, spiritual, societal and political discussions are going on within Muslim communities all over the world.

In fact, to the degree that we can speak of 'a Muslim world' and 'a Christian world',[4] the current states of these two worlds are

[4] Concepts like 'the Islamic World', 'the Christian World', 'the East' or 'the West' can, of course, only be used within an abundance of nuance. Considering their constant interaction throughout the last 1,400 years of history, they never were as separated as people often tend to think. When such terms are used in this book,

significantly different when it comes to the volatility of the cultural,
theological and philosophical debates. The Christian world is a lot
more docile. Except for some symbolic discussions on topics like
abortion or creationism, the influence of Christianity as an
intellectual, theological and ethical force within the societal debates
is much smaller.

This is not to say that innovating Christian theology, certainly on
an academic level, does not exist. This also is not to say that
spirituality has no place in present day Western societies. However,
by and large, the Christian world has subordinated the theological
and spiritual discussions to more secular principles. It has forfeited
primacy to politics and economics. Spirituality and religion have
been pushed to the back and into the private sphere. Put
differently, 'minding God's presence' is not much of an attribute of
the public intellectual debate.

This is quite different in the Muslim world. The debates on how to
shape society in line with certain spiritual realities are very much at
the forefront. This does not, however, imply that all these ideas
and proposals would inevitably lead to some strict implementation
of religious edicts or the imposition of a theocracy. Quite the
contrary. In many circles, a heightened sense of religious and
spiritual belonging goes hand in hand with a plea for democracy
and human rights.

On every level, people are involved in these discussions. Scholars
in the old academic strongholds of a university such as Al-Azhar in
Cairo writing treatises on Qur'anic exegesis, youngsters in migrant
communities of Berlin seeking novel ways to construe their hybrid
identities, politicians in Islamabad who claim a connection to
mystical traditions — all of them are debating the manner in which
religion, spirituality, society and politics can find an equilibrium.

Sure, certain voices might sound louder for various reasons and

---

they simply are what they are; that is to say, broad generalizations. As such, they
certainly still leave room for plenty of specific counterexamples.

the loudest voices often are not the most sensible ones, but eventually no single voice can claim hegemony. Some would like to strangle every form of discussion and often succeed very well, but the fact of the matter is that they are incapable of doing so continuously. Therefore, one of the most intriguing social evolutions of previous years, as well as in years to come, is this global discussion within the Muslim community.

———— ✺ ————

All religious traditions have known several periods of vibrancy, stagnation and rigidity. Thus, no one needs to deny that much of the contemporary Muslim world is quite stuck within the confines of the bond between religious patriarchy and despotic politics. At the same time, it is buzzing all over, for in today's global debates, Islam is pressured on all sides. Just like a volcano that is stirred when the layers of the earth underneath start moving, it erupts. Furthermore, within the lava that is being spewed out, not only the worst but also the very best are brought to the surface.

Perhaps that is why my own journey through Islam really took off in New York, the very city that witnessed the act which engrained the 'clash of civilisations' in the global politics; and actually, not just in New York, but in the office of Imam Feisal Abdul Rauf, the spiritual leader of the so-called 'Ground Zero Mosque'.

As some might remember, in 2010, a heated and heavily politicized media-debate arose around the plans to build a Muslim community centre close to the emptiness where the Twin Towers once stood. The discussion went on for several weeks and stirred the international press.

In a sense, the Ground Zero Mosque controversy was heavily symbolic. It perfectly reflected the state of the global debates on Islam. Although the sensitivity of some critics might have been understandable, they paid no attention to the fact that the centre was not actually going to be a mosque but rather a 'Cordoba

House' — a place where people could meet other people of different faiths in a spirit of openness and dialogue. Their fear of 'Muslim extremism creeping up on them' completely blinded them to the fact that Imam Feisal is one of the exponents of the new and contemporary reinterpretations of Islam. He's one of those interesting voices in the discussions on the manner in which tradition and modernity might be reconciled.

*Photo by Enid Bloch*

# FEISAL ABDUL RAUF
## ON FAITH, FEAR AND LOVE

*Feisal Abdul Rauf is the sort of religious leader that gets asked to give a lecture at the World Economic Forum at Davos. In 1997, he founded the American Society for Muslim Advancement (ASMA), he has been Imam of Masjid al-Farah in New York City, he sits on the Board of Trustees of the Islamic Center of New York and he is the chairman of the Cordoba Initiative, a multi-national, multi-faith organization dedicated to improving understanding and building trust among people of all cultures and religions.*

*The latter quickly brought us to the topic of fear and love – not only on the fear and love of Islam within society, but also on the fear and love of God within ourselves.*

———— ❁ ————

**In the whole debate around the Park 51 project, which some people called the 'Ground Zero Mosque', tensions rose quite high. Consequently, your message often got lost. Yet, if you'd like to summarise that message in all quietness, how would you phrase it?**

Given the misperception of people that Islam is a religion of terrorism and exclusiveness, the biggest thing I would like people to know is that Islam is a religion of love, peace and compassion.

That is why one of my books is called *Moving the Mountain*. I want to move the mountain of suspicion. I want to remove the mountain of misunderstandings of Islam. I want to remove the myths that people have of Islam as a religion that it is negative and violent. I wish to get rid of the image – shared even by Muslims – that there is only one right interpretation of Islam.

**An honourable goal, to say the least, but not an easy task. The fear of Islam seems to envelop ever more people.**

Islamophobia is, indeed, on the rise, but I think that acceptance of Islam is as well. What is important, however, is that we develop an 'American Islam' – or a Belgian Islam, a French Islam and a German Islam for that matter. What I mean by that is not that the theology would be different, but that the jurisprudence, the laws, the cultures and the practices would vary according to the context.
I base this upon the history of Islam itself. Islam spread from Arabia to Egypt to Byzantium to Persia to India to Africa. And it expressed itself in all of those cultures through different forms of architecture, calligraphy and music. So, we as American Muslims – or European Muslims – also need to develop a personal American Muslim – or European – identity that expresses itself through the culture of our context.

**As far as I can see, this cultural reinterpretation of Islam is already happening. Many people look for new ways to adapt the basic essence of Islamic living and practice to the new contexts of the modern world. Yet, I mostly perceive it within migrant communities. Although many migrants still look towards the scholars of the East, I have the feeling that a lot of novel ways of thinking about Islam come from Muslim scholars in the West.**

You are right about that. In the West, there is a lot of intellectual and academic freedom. Muslim scholars in the West can write more freely. Look at someone like Rashid Al-Ghanoushi, who was previously living in the UK. He returned to Tunisia after the revolutions of the Arab Spring, but before he could only express himself freely from the UK. That is, in fact, why he said that the UK is an Islamic state. In doing so, he referred to an element of Islamic law to back up his argument since the classical definition of *Dar al-Islam*[5] calls any country a part of the Dar al-Islam where Muslims can perform their prayers, can go to the Friday sermons freely and can bury the dead in Muslim cemeteries. So yes, it is in the West that many new ideas and initiatives are surfacing and the West can, indeed, be viewed as a part of Dar al-Islam.

**You belong to a Sufi brotherhood yourself. Do you see a specific place for *Sufism* in the many changes the Dar al-Islam is going through at the moment?[6]**

Sufism exists all over the world, and I think it's an important part of our faith since it is the spiritual dimension of our faith.

In any authentic spirituality there is an experience of God. As a Muslim, I'm supposed to 'bear witness there is a God'. But how do I 'bear witness'? Unless I learn to experience his existence spiritually, all I'm doing is acting like a parrot – repeating words. So for me, it's through Sufism that you gain a genuine experience of

---

[5] Literally 'Dar al-Islam' means 'the House of Islam'. It is a term used to refer to the 'world of Islam' or, put differently, those areas in the world where Islam is practiced.
[6] Sufism is commonly referred to as 'Islamic mysticism' but, although it's a very popular aspect of the Islamic tradition in the West, it is often very misunderstood. In my conversations with Peter Sanders, Abdal Hakim Murad, Abdulwahid Van Bommel, Kudsi Ergüner and Dr. D. Latifa, I go much deeper into the concept of Islamic mysticism and the misconceptions surrounding it. But at the time when I met Imam Feisal, I had not yet grasped certain elements of the Islamic tradition in general and of Islamic mysticism in particular. The manner in which I posed the question thus reveals how I still lacked a more thorough comprehension of its particular (and very important) place within Islamic spirituality.

the faith.

## Do you then see the mystical dimension as the common ground between religions?

Mysticism can be such a common ground, but there's much common ground on the ethical level as well. The golden rule, "do not do unto others what you do not want others to do to you", has come to all religions and, thus, offers a very powerful basis for commonality. On top of it, within Abrahamic religions, there is of course also the belief in one God. So, there are actually a whole lot of different elements that offer possibilities for a deep rapprochement.

And the differences, well, those should be celebrated. It's not because you're Belgian you can't enjoy Turkish kebab or Baklava. And the same is true for music, rituals and so on. Most things simply aren't exclusive.

## Considering there is so much common ground, how then do you reflect upon those situations in certain countries where converting to another faith as a Muslim is penalized – sometimes even with a death sentence?

That is simply wrong. It's an incorrect interpretation of old laws. Every instance where, in the Prophet's time, conversion was related with the death penalty went together with treason. It happened during a time of war between Medina and Mecca, where apostasy wasn't just apostasy. It was treason because they were people who had first left the community and then fought against the community. That kind of treason has always been a capital crime – even in the United States. But when the Prophet finally made a treaty and peace with Mecca, he even agreed in writing that anybody who had left the Muslim community could peacefully go back. That is why one of my friends, who's a judge in the high court in Pakistan, says apostasy simpliciter, that is to say, the act of leaving one's faith community is not a punishable crime. Of course it is the biggest sin and God will punish it in the hereafter, but we have no authority to enact any punishment. Just like it is a sin not to pray, not to fast, to eat pork, and so on. Those aren't sins that we can punish because they aren't sins that hurt anybody. The only sins which are punishable on earth are the sins that hurt people, like killing and stealing.

**Do you truly believe that God, in the hereafter, will in fact punish those people that were Muslim but converted to another faith when they found love and light in that faith?**

I personally believe that whoever follows his conscience is a Muslim in God's eyes. You can be a Muslim in the sense of 'following the tradition of the Prophet', but that is not entirely the same as being *a believer in God*. A real Muslim is 'someone that submits'. So, the person that believes in God and the last day and does good has nothing to worry about because God defines your religion upon your belief in Him and your ethics. What you call yourself is immaterial.

**I hear a plea for a religion of genuineness, lived from the heart and soul . . . As a contemporary Christian, I can, of course, relate very easily to the idea of sincere faith and ethics as the basis of religion, but within the Qur'an, one also constantly encounters the concept of *taqwa*, which is mostly translated as 'the fear of God'. And that's a concept I am less acquainted with. It used to exist, of course, within the Christian tradition, but today it's less at the forefront. Even more so, it seems rather counter-intuitive to my perception of God as an infinite source of love. How do you, as a Muslim, reconcile the love for God and the fear of God?**

Fear and love are in fact flipsides of the same coin. When you love someone very much, you fear hurting them. And when you've done something wrong that might hurt the one you love, you feel bad about it and fear the reaction. So, the more you love God, the more you fear doing something bad. When you're going to the office of a very powerful person, you want their love, but you also fear their office and their power. And God is the absolute power.

It is like when you see somebody who is so tremendously intelligent or magnificently beautiful that whatever is in you somehow submits and prostrates in front of that person. I remember meeting such a person at Colombia University who I thought was an absolute genius and I could feel my mind and my brain somehow prostrate and bow down in front of his brilliance. So, it is a positive fear that makes your heart go into prostration when you see an immense amount of beauty.

In fact, 'taqwa' means 'to protect yourself'. As such, it does not just mean 'fear of God', but also 'to protect yourself from God'. It's a bit like the sun. We love the sun, but if you sit in the sun too long, you get sunburned. So, however much you want to be in the sun, you also have to apply a bit of lotion to protect yourself. And God is more radiant than a million suns. So, if you don't fear the intensity of the divine, you will get burned. That's why God says: 'watch out, beware of my power and protect yourself'. He even tells us which lotion to put on to protect ourselves: 'be good, love one another', and so on. The spiritual ethics of religion are the protecting lotion of the believer.

***. . . Imam Feisal pauses a bit, there is some silence and then he adds . . .***

You know, the word 'love' is difficult. When you say, 'I love döner kebab', 'I love Mozart', 'I love Armani' or 'I love my wife', you use the same word 'love', but what does it really mean? What is the dynamic? What is the interaction? When I say, 'I love my wife', it doesn't mean I'll cook her, chop her up and eat her like a döner kebab. So what is love? Love is a function of the lover and the beloved. And the nature of the dynamic can be different even though we use the same word. So when we say we love God, what does it mean? How do we love God? Is it the way you love your wife? The way you love Mozart? The way you love döner kebab? We use words like love, fear, surrender and so on, but in the context of God, they have much more complex meanings. They have much richer and deeper meanings. And they have a bigger spectrum of meanings because God is the source of everything. So, when you use this terminology of 'loving God' and 'fearing God', it's more than loving your wife, music, food, mathematics, novels and so on, and yet, it has aspects of all of that.

# IMAN

The word '*iman*' is often translated as 'belief'. It refers to the acceptance of certain metaphysical premises of the Muslim faith. It's mostly summarized in six articles: belief in God, belief in the angels, belief in divine books, belief in the prophets, belief in the Day of Judgment and belief in God's predestination.

This iman cannot be equated with something like the Nicean Creed in Christianity, however, for although many Muslims might attest to these six aspects of iman, they are not the core essence of their faith. The core essence of the Muslim faith is fully contained within one sentence called the *shahada*: "There is no God but *the* God and Muhammad is a prophet of God." Voicing this shahada in a genuine way is enough to become a Muslim.[7]

On the other hand, the shahada is only one of the so-called five pillars of Islam. The other pillars, however, aren't aspects of faith. They are 'ritual acts': praying five times a day, fasting once a year, giving alms to the poor and making an effort to go on a pilgrimage to Mecca at least once in your life.

In this regard, the tradition of Islam differs quite strongly from Christianity. Within Christianity, faith in a certain set of premises is the quintessential prerequisite of being religious. That is to say, to

---

[7] The content of the shahada will be discussed more profoundly from p. 217 and onwards.

be a Christian, one needs to believe in a series of concepts. In Islam, however, the essence of the faith is expressed in one simple sentence while the rest of one's religiosity is dependent on the way it is practiced.

In scholarly terms, this is referred to as the difference between orthodoxy and orthopraxy. Orthodoxy places its strongest emphasis on correct teachings and truths, while orthopraxy places its strongest emphasis on correct actions.

Obviously, Christianity is not devoid of rituals and there has always been much theological debate on how 'proper faith' should bring a believer to 'proper action'. Just as obviously, Islam is also not solely occupied with 'proper action' since the greatest 'act' and the most important pillar is an act of faith. However, understanding the difference between orthodoxy and orthopraxy remains quite useful to see how this difference in their basic religious attitude gave way to very different realities.

What binds Christians throughout the world – whether Protestant, Catholic, Anglicans or Orthodox – will eventually be the things they believe in and the manner in which these beliefs shape their values. What binds Muslims throughout the world is much more their ritual acts, such as praying towards Mecca five times a day and the manner in which they come together during the *hajj*.[8]

The differences in the theological, social and spiritual views of Muslims can, therefore, be quite huge. Of course, it is undeniable that certain groups somehow deem it necessary to convince all other Muslims of particular theological interpretations and brandish those who don't share their views as heretics. Yet, because of the very premises Islam is built upon, it is actually quite difficult to brandish any Muslim as a heretic. No matter what someone else might say or think, as long as you can say the shahada and somehow uphold some or all of the rituals, you

---

[8] The hajj is the pilgrimage to Mecca, which Muslims are supposed to perform at least once in their lifetime if physically and financially able.

actually remain a Muslim.

———— ✹ ————

All of this brings about a seeming paradox that is often difficult to understand from a Christian perspective: although many Muslims will often refer to the '*Ummah*',[9] the worldwide Muslim community, there is actually very little that defines something like 'a Muslim identity'. As such, it is not because someone says he's a Muslim or belongs to the Ummah that one can know what his beliefs are or how he exactly expresses his religion.

This becomes very clear in many migrant communities which are spread out over much of the Western and Christian world. In those communities, questions about what it means to belong to the Ummah or what exactly a Muslim identity might entail have risen to the forefront.

These questions did not just pop up, however, nor are they the result of some simple process of 'radicalisation'. They came about because of a crucial shift in the public debates that pushed Muslim youngsters to question their identity. One of those shifts was the fact that the host societies gradually stopped framing migrants within their ethnic or national background and increasingly connected them to their religion. That is to say, instead of seeing them as Turks, Moroccans, Egyptians or Pakistanis, they started to identify them as Muslims. Many Muslims then started to do the same. They did so partly as a reaction to the changing public rhetoric and partly because many migrants of the third and fourth generation have lost their bonds with the home countries of their (great-)grandfathers. The youth of various minority groups thus

---

[9] Ummah is an Arabic word which means 'nation' or 'community'. It is distinguished from Sha'b which means a nation with common ancestry or geography. As such, Ummah refers to a community that is not bound by lineage or place and has, by now, become synonymous with the worldwide Muslim community.

often feel connected to one another because of the fact that they're Muslim.

But within these migrant Muslim communities and within their collective search for identity, one can find all strands of social and political thought, from the most conservative to the most liberal, from the most authoritarian to the most democratic.

──────── ✿ ────────

Most certainly, one can find just as great a variety of socio-political thought within the Christian world but, as was already touched upon in the chapter on 'Islam',[10] what makes the search for identity within the migrant communities so interesting is the manner in which they are seeking ways to retain traditions within the modern world.

This, of course, has a lot to do with the Islamic tendency towards orthopraxy. Whatever philosophical or ideological school they belong too, Muslims all over the world have always sought ways to implement traditions and practices into their daily lives. That's still true today. Whatever social or political mindset they might have, many groups and individuals are seeking novel ways to fuse age old practices and rituals with contemporary world views.

In this respect, I was quite charmed by Cyrus McGoldrick, a.k.a. the Raskol Khan. Cyrus is an adamant human rights activist but with a look that might easily stir the prejudices of his American neighbours. As a perfect example of contemporary hybridity, he's a fervent advocate of his faith by day and an inspiring hip hop artist by night.

─────────────────────

[10] See p. 25 and onwards.

*Photo by Ariane Moshayedi*

# CYRUS MCGOLDRICK
## ON ACTIVISM, IDENTITY AND
## RIGHTEOUS ANGER

*Cyrus McGoldrick is an American Muslim of Iranian and Irish descent who worked at several civil rights organisations that fight against discrimination, such as CAIR, the Council on American-Islamic Relations, NCPCF, the National Coalition to Protect Civil Freedom and the Youth Coalition of South Florida.*

*Cyrus' work as a human-rights activist, in fact, smoothly mixes with his artistic alter ego: the Raskol Khan. For many years, he's been recording and performing his fusion of faith and hip hop for an ever growing fan base both within and outside the US. Yet, even though Islam is the focus of both his work and his music, Cyrus wasn't raised as a Muslim. "A lot of people think that my Islam comes from my Iranian roots. But no, I took a rather 'scenic route'," he told me at the start of our very amicable conversation. My interest was immediately aroused.*

———— ❈ ————

**What kind of 'scenic route' was that?**

I was raised loosely Christian, but my parents weren't dogmatic about it. In fact, they got married three times: once in city hall, once in a mosque and once in a church. They wanted to make sure

it certainly counted, I guess. *(Cyrus laughs.)*
In our conversations about spiritual stuff, the focus was always on God and service – on being good, telling the truth and helping the community. But I actually wasn't into religion when I was young.
It wasn't until college that I started researching more about religion. At first, my interest was more the politics and anthropology of it, and then, when I eventually got into the spiritual side of it as well, the first book that had a real impact on me was the Bhagavad-Gita.[11] For the first time, I felt the unity of creation. It all made sense to me and it all started to connect. It didn't settle me on Hinduism, however. I continued searching and even got to a point where I was reading the Qur'an as well as trying to meditate, and none of it well. But, after a while, all the pieces started to come together and I simply realized Islam was the religion for me. There wasn't any special epiphany. I just kind of flowed into Islam and I've always been very fulfilled by it.

**I've read the Bhagavad-Gita numerous times myself and I would say that, in many ways, it's a lot more 'approachable' than the Qur'an, at least for a Western public. To read the Qur'an, I always think you need quite a lot of theological background to be able to grasp it properly. How come it clicked with you?**

When I started learning more about Islam, the first thing my teacher told me to read wasn't the Qur'an, but a biography of the Prophet. And he was right to do that, because first we have to trust the sources. While learning more about the Prophet's life, I came to realize why it's obvious that the revelation came to him specifically. He's the model of how to live according to the revelation. That's why my teacher also said that someone who's losing faith should read the biography of the Prophet and not

---

[11] The Bhagavad-Gita is one of the most important spiritual books in the Hindu traditions.

necessarily the Qur'an. The Qur'an should be approached with the proper mindset and respect. If I don't get something out of it, it's my problem, not the problem of the book.

**All of this explains how you became a Muslim, but how did an Irish-Iranian young man get into the hip hop scene?**

When I came to New York, trying to adjust and find my way, I started playing music with friends, went to rooftop parties in Brooklyn, got involved with some bands, and before I knew it, some people that were light years ahead of me in experience got me to write some lyrics and record them. So, there I was, a bit of a 'Caucasian anomaly' among hip hop, reggae and calypso musicians, but I felt I became good at it and I got a lot of encouragement. At first I didn't take it too seriously, but when I went traveling through Europe, I saw some great music, particularly folk bands, that really got to me and made me think about my own direction. An artist, to me, should have a kind of a 'persona', a style that differentiates his character and I wondered what that could be for me. In the years that followed, the Raskol Khan was born.

**So how would you describe that 'persona' of the Raskol Khan?**

Mainstream hip hop is based on that idea of consumption and waste. It's about being proud that we can buy the waste, the poison that's being sold to us. Hip hop started as an antagonistic and oppositional culture, but it got taken up by the mainstream culture and became a part of it and even started selling its materialism as something positive. The Raskol Khan is my way of starting from that point and then undermining it. I wanted to show that I was a victim of it as well and share my learning process. I haven't always been a nice person. I haven't always been spiritual. I've been a knucklehead, too. And the Raskol Khan offers me a way to express my experiences of what I've been through because I can use the music as a sort of common ground, yet once again, as a form of opposition.

**You don't look like a hip hop artist, however. As the Raskol Khan, you retain a very Islamic image.**

You know, in American Islam, we don't have too many role models outside of religious scholarship. Even the Muslims who do get some fame in the corporate world or the mainstream culture usually don't look like me or most Muslims. They're the ones that totally fit in, that pass. They gave up certain parts of their identity in order to succeed in others. And I don't mean to demonize them, but it seems important to me that we also have some role models who practice Islam and who are proud of the external aspects of their identity. Otherwise, every time you see somebody on the news that looks like me, he wasn't up to much good. It distorts the image. So, I kind of wanted to reclaim that as well.

Therefore, if I can boil down my music into two things, it's reclaiming our religion and reclaiming our right to dissent. I'm pretty comfortable in that role and I'm going to stay in it because I realized that every individual is the battleground of everyone else's rights.

**So activism and advocacy are also a part of being the Raskol Khan?**

It was, in fact, a turning point for me to figure out how I could use the Raskol Khan as a platform to get some messages across. Before that, I had ideas to express, but I didn't like being on stage. My first inclination was to record, throw it online and let people listen to it. I didn't want to be in the spotlight and draw attention to myself because it felt a bit awkward. But then one day I realized: "In one hand, I have a cause I deeply care about, and in the other,

I have a stage and a spotlight . . . Perhaps I don't have to talk about myself but I can put the message in the spotlight and let it speak for itself." So I started seeing it as an educational opportunity both for the audience and myself.

It's not all just politics though. To me, it's more about ethics in the broader sense. I've never been able to disconnect faith and activism because, at the end of the day, I think it's about service and human dignity. If, in any way, you believe that there's a law higher than the law of the jungle, then we have something in common. So, I'm not going to try to convert anybody. I'd rather have people be a good Christian than a bad Muslim.

Imam Ali, the fourth *caliph*[12] said: "Every person is either your brother in faith, or your brother in humanity." A lot of people throw around the word 'Ummah' recklessly, however. They think it simply means 'the Muslim community'. That's a good way to think about it but not the only way. We need to get past the community ego a bit because we're all in this together. To me, the Ummah is the greater humanity and that's what we should be focused on.

**In your daily work, you have a strong focus on human rights. Is there a lot of need in the US for an organization like CAIR or the NCPCF? Do Muslims encounter a lot of violations of their civil rights?**

Our work is most certainly needed. To give you an example, the research of some journalists once exposed a covert surveillance program within our police department. The New York Police Department keeps files on every Friday sermon of all the mosques in New York and beyond. Sometimes they tape it, sometimes it's just informants listening and taking notes. Muslims are closely watched in the US, in our schools, businesses, even homes, and anyone saying something a bit 'different' might get a visit from the

---

[12] A caliph is a successor of the Prophet and, thus, a leader of the Muslim community.

police or the FBI. It should be no surprise then that a lot of Muslims have internalized the feeling of 'being watched all the time'.[13]

One of the very strange things in this post 9/11 era is that religious behaviour got criminalized. In 2007, the NYPD released a document called 'Radicalization in the West', written by some former CIA agents. That document alleges that every Muslim can somehow become a fully mobilized home grown terrorist. And the supposed signs of becoming a terrorist are things like growing a beard, frequenting mosques, going to bookstores and giving up smoking. So, in their logic, it's only normal that they put surveillance on all mosques because everybody who's practicing a religion is a potential threat.

I used to want to say it's all a misunderstanding, but it's difficult to still believe that because it's gone way too far. It's all part of the war-machine and we have to wake up to it.

We're a very polarized country at the moment. Everybody used to run to the middle but these days it's the Tea Party at one end and then a fragmented Left, but that Left is pretty much disconnected from mainstream institutions. So, there's not much media speaking on our behalf or telling the truth as we know it.

**In any polarized situation, the extremes amplify each other. So what about the rise of extremist ideas on the Muslim side in the US?**

Some young people do tend to seek extremes in Islam and other ideologies. But the feeling that the so-called extremists actually feed on is the desire we have to save the world. Everyone is waiting for their letter from Hogwarts that shows them their destiny. That's why they often leave their communities. They might

---

[13] One or two years after my conversation with Cyrus McGoldrick, the city of New York disbanded this controversial surveillance program. As a historic example, it does remain very relevant of course.

still come to the mosques to pray but they don't belong to the group anymore, partly because the group can't handle their energy and partly because the youth see that the imams aren't addressing the real issues, like the injustices done by the government or the worldwide oppression the Muslim community is going through.

So, if our spiritual leaders don't dare to address crucial issues, and just want to wrap themselves in an American flag to appease others, we will lose a lot of good kids.

We need to be honest and dare to address the difficult issues. We should also talk about the idea of *jihad*,[14] for example, or about what it means to be a *mujahid*.[15] We need to explain how those concepts are realistic, but also above terrorism and have different, authentic meanings. Because if we don't talk about it, they'll go and listen to others who aren't necessarily the right people. If you act as if the idea of jihad doesn't exist in Islam, they'll know you don't know what you're talking about and run to Internet *shaykhs*[16] or others to find some answers that might lead them astray.

We don't need to tell young kids – like some imams and speakers do – that they shouldn't be outspoken. There really isn't any need to water down our religion just to seem nice, because we can be truthful to our religion as well as outspoken and still find a lot that connects us to people of other faiths. One of those things is, for example, that it's not only your Islamic duty but also your patriotic duty to uplift society to the best of your abilities.

---

[14] It is often thought that the term jihad refers to some sort of obligatory 'holy war' but jihad actually means 'striving'. It can, therefore, indeed be used in the context of battle, but it can just as well designate the spiritual effort to become a better human being. A more elaborate explanation about the term can be found on p. 175.

[15] A mujahid is someone who's 'involved' in jihad; that is to say, someone who struggles on the path of Allah.

[16] The word shaykh is often wrongly associated with rich Arab businessmen. It's actually an honorific that literally means 'elder' and which is given to someone who's the leader of a community. As such, it might refer to the leader of a tribe or clan in a political sense, but in a religious sense, it will refer to the spiritual leader of a particular religious community.

**Is that also a message you try to bring through your music?**

Sure. When I'm on stage or when I speak, I try to bring the message that I'm not here to water it down, that I'm not here to tell anyone how they need to dress or that they should be more 'Western' — whatever that means. No, I only want to tell them: "you need to be you".

Just recently, a student came to me after a panel discussion and said: "You know . . . you're the first person I met who says it's okay to be angry". That made my day because what brought me into Islam was, in fact, a sense of social justice.

**I can understand that very well. I personally think we often forget that there are two types of anger: the egoistic one and the spiritual one. The latter is like Jesus' anger when he whipped the merchants out of the temple.**

Yeah, righteous anger! There simply is no peace without justice, or at least no lasting peace. There weren't many ethnic or cultural conflicts under Saddam Hussein, for example, but that was because he was doing the killing. You can enforce peace but then it isn't real peace.

We always have to remember it's about love — even when we talk about anger and justice. I don't tell people not to be angry and upset, because frankly, if you're not angry and upset with certain things happening in the world, then you're not paying attention. But that kind of anger comes from love, from wanting to protect your loved ones from injustice.

# IHSAN

There's a story in the tradition of Islam that recounts how the angel Gabriel once visited the Prophet and asked him: "What is *Ihsan?*" Muhammad answered: "It is that you should serve Allah as though you could see Him, for though you cannot see Him, He sees you."

Ihsan is often called the last of the three dimensions of the Islamic religion. The other two are Islam ('spiritual submission' as it is expressed in the five pillars)[17] and iman (the six aspects of faith).[18] Ihsan, then, actually combines Islam and iman. That is to say, ihsan is the coherence between your faith and your actions.

That is why ihsan can be translated as 'perfection' or 'excellence' as well as 'to do beautiful things'. So, in line with the difference between orthodoxy and orthopraxy, the envisioned result of Islam as religion is not so much a matter of 'knowing the truth' as it is of 'being a good person'.

In this respect, it is interesting to see how the Christian tradition has such a strong focus on 'knowing the truth' even though it's most basic belief is the incarnation of God.

Within Islam on the other hand, just like in Judaism, God cannot be portrayed. There is no image, let alone an 'embodiment' of

---

[17] See p. 25.
[18] See p. 39.

God. Traditionally speaking, even the Prophet shouldn't be portrayed in order to prevent people from worshipping the Prophet besides God.[19] Nonetheless, many Muslims will try to conform to the Prophet since he is considered to be the most pure example of ihsan. In their effort of trying to be a good person, many Muslims will, therefore, try to be 'like the Prophet' (sometimes overdoing it so much that one can actually question whether it doesn't come close to worship). In fact, this might sound quite a lot like the Christian concept of 'imitatio Christi', i.e. of imitating Jesus, but within Christianity, this concept remained a smaller and lesser known aspect of the broader tradition.

This brings about the strange and quite ironic situation where many Christians today will have a rather ambivalent relationship towards trinity and often don't know what to make of Christ's divinity, while many Muslims have a tendency to almost deify Muhammad.

All in all, this simply shows how difficult it can be to find the proper balance between faith and action, between letter and spirit, between image and content.

---

Images are easily distorted and distorted images often trigger conflicts. A distorted image of God can be used to suppress people and a distorted image of religion can be used to wage wars. But both Christianity and Islam also have ways of 'going beyond the images', of seeking truth and bringing it to the surface, of experiencing a deeper beauty and somehow portraying the unseen.

To reflect some more on these matters, I turned to Peter Sanders, a renowned photographer of the Muslim world.

---

[19] Contrary to what most people think, however, this certainly isn't an absolute rule. One can easily find depictions and portraits of Muhammad. This was often done in devotional contexts, such as on cards and drawings that were being sold in the vicinity of holy places.

*Photo by John Gulliver*

# PETER SANDERS
## ON IMAGES OF ISLAM

*Peter Sanders was one of the very first Europeans to take photographs of Mecca and Medina. To get permission proved to be quite a bureaucratic task back in 1971, but luckily he succeeded for his impressive pictures eventually found their way into Stern, Paris Match, the Observer, the Sunday Times and other important periodicals. As such, the Western world was given a fresh look into the heart of Islam.*

*When he started out as a photographer, however, he mainly took pictures of the rock icons of the sixties, such as Jimi Hendrix, the Rolling Stones, Bob Dylan, the Doors and The Who – to name but a few.*

———— ❀ ————

**How did you find your way from the glamour of the world of rock to Islam?**

In the beginning of the seventies, I became more interested in spirituality and went to India, which was quite the fashion in those days. During the seven months I spent there, I studied most religions, though I read only a little bit about Islam. When I came back, however, I noticed how some of the people that I knew from the music business had become Muslim, while others had gotten heavily into drugs, black magic and other things. So, I felt I was being pointed in a pretty clear direction.

As I was thinking over what to do next, someone told me more about Sufism. He explained to me how the structure of Islam is like a house but that you need to have a spiritual heart at the centre of that house. *Tasawwuf*[20] was that spiritual heart, he said. If you take it out of the house, you don't have the protection, but if you only keep the outer shell, you lose the real spirit. That analogy made sense to me. So I took some sort of a 'leap of faith' and felt that Islam was the right path for me. I quickly set off for Morocco and spent a month with a shaykh called Shaykh Muhammad ibn al Habib. Three months later, I began a journey to Saudi Arabia to perform the hajj. After obtaining permission, I took those pictures of the hajj that were so well received worldwide. Since then, I have been traveling all over the world, photographing Muslims and their Islamic culture.

**The relationship between Islam and the creation of images hasn't always been too easy. So, did you have a spiritual conflict between your job and the religion you had gone into? Certainly if one considers you photographed people, perhaps it might have brought you some doubt?**

To be honest, it was simply what I did, so I didn't see much of a problem. After a while, I of course became aware that some Muslims disapproved. I tried to understand their point of view, but what I arrived at eventually is that the prohibition of making images of people is about three-dimensional idols. A photograph, however, is like looking at your face in the mirror or seeing a reflection in a pond. I wasn't recreating something that wasn't there – neither did I use the pictures for worship.

Another thing is that I have often photographed people who were much evolved spiritually as well as scholastically. They never

---

[20] Tasawwuf is the inner, spiritual and mystical dimension of Islam.

refused to let me take their picture. If it was so wrong, why would these people let me do it? On top of it, those people who came up to me and said that photography is forbidden in Islam, well, when I discussed this with them, I could sense that their whole nature was very narrow, often very judgmental and usually not very scholarly. So, until someone can come up with a proof that I can accept, I will not mind.

**The Qur'an, in fact, often mentions how God's signs can be perceived all around us. In a sense, these passages remind us that God shows himself through the beauty of creation. Is such a thought one of the inspirations behind your work?**

I would even add that the Qur'an also says: 'Look at the signs within yourself and on the horizon.' These two dimensions are present all the time. There's the outward world we're experiencing and there's what's happening to you inwardly. Those two things have to play together. These days, however, a lot of Muslims have become very literal in their approach to Islam and they have forgotten the inner dimension. But that inner dimension was my focus from the start. I've spent my life looking at creation, contemplating it and trying to understand it.

That's also what I try to teach at my photographic workshops. We, that is, myself and all those supporting me in the effort, call our workshops 'the art of seeing' because they're not so much about the technical side of photography as they are about relearning how to look at what surrounds us. People are often just so busy with their lives that they forget to sometimes just stop and look.

Photography is about 'tuning into the moment'. You have to still the self so you can be in a state to really see things. Otherwise your mind is always chattering away. That blocks your vision. You have to learn to calm yourself down.

**If you ask me, this does not only apply to photographers. The**

**whole of society should learn to 'calm the mind to really see things'.**

Indeed, but it's all a complex matter, of course. We, for example, can't say that this minority of people who fuel the radical and distorted view of Islam don't exist. And the trouble with such a type of minority is that they always shout very loud so everybody becomes aware of them, while what I call 'the silent majority' tends to remain unnoticed.

In fact, I think the silent majority, including myself, have to discover what real Islam is. And above all, we have to *be* Islam. We can't say 'Islam is peace' and then as soon as something goes wrong in our lives start to rant and yell. Nobody is going to believe Islam is peace if we're not peaceful beings ourselves. I often wonder what would happen if ten thousand Muslims went out for a protest, sat down, were quiet, behaved well and perhaps chanted prayers. A bit like the Buddhists – they're often a better example of that peace than we are. So, I really don't understand why Muslims so quickly have the feeling that they have to scream and shout. It doesn't change anything, it doesn't help the situation.

But how do you affect all those things? I don't really know. Like I said, the challenge Islam is facing is that we will have to *be* our Islam. That's also how Islam spread: by the example of spiritually evolved people who were kind and compassionate. They had all those amazing qualities that you can find in any great person of any religion.

**In a way, you're saying that people should become an 'image' of their own spirituality . . .**

Yes, and related to that, I am in fact working on a project called *Meetings with Mountains*. Some people laugh when I talk about it again. I've been working on it for forty years, but I am actually now close to completing it.[21] The end result will be a book that brings together the photographs of the different saints and evolved spiritual leaders that I had the good fortune to meet while traveling throughout the Muslim world. So, whenever I heard of a great shaykh or scholar, I would go to meet him to hear his wise words and to photograph him. Some of them have never been photographed before. Not that they had a problem with photography but they are extremely humble in nature and, as such, stay away from anything that might exalt them.

One reason I really wanted to bring together all these great people is because it's a spiritual side of Islam that has almost never been presented. Within every religion, there have always been saintly people, but somehow many people don't think you can also find them within Islam. And even many Muslims don't know about them since they don't seek fame and because of that, they often remain hidden.

**There is, of course, a bit of a contradiction in such a project. The whole world is so focused on 'image' and 'fame' that there's indeed a great need to spread the message of those humble spiritual people. Yet, in order to do so, you need to show their images and, thus, you actually bring them some sort of 'fame'.**

That's true, but on the other hand, as I said, it took me many years to collect all the photographs. And by now a lot of them have died. A friend of mine once said that this might be exactly why they let me photograph them, because they knew that they would be gone and could leave a bit of their legacy in my hands. So, I just feel it is needed, not to give them fame but to let people know that they exist and to make people aware that we can gain spiritual benefit simply by being in their company.

---

[21] We had our conversation on the 21st of October, 2012.

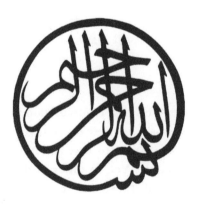

# TRADITIONAL
# ESSENTIALS

# QUR'AN

When we would like to allow a new and more thorough image of Islam within our reflections and debates, an obvious question quickly arises: where can we go to find such a more accurate image and who can we consult to deepen our understanding? In other words, what are the sources and who are the authorities we can turn to?

When it comes to the sources, it's rather self-evident that one should at least read the Qur'an. Yet, even though the primacy of the Qur'an is an undeniable given within Islam, Christians don't completely understand the true significance of that holy book since they tend to equate the Qur'an with the Bible and, in line with this comparison, tend to equate Muhammad with Jesus. However, this is a significant misunderstanding. If we want to make a true comparison, we should equate the Qur'an with Christ instead of the Bible.

Perhaps this might sound bizarre at first but, in the end, it makes more sense. Within Christianity, Christ Himself is the revelation and the New Testament 'testifies' of this living revelation, while in Islam, the Prophet is nothing but an ordinary man — a man that truly lived virtuously, but, nevertheless, was simply human. And this human was given a revelation which was eventually written down in the Qur'an. The Qur'an then is the essence of the Islamic revelation and not Muhammad.

Obviously, this basic difference brings about a lot of other essential theological differences between the two faiths. Muslims, for example, cannot accept Christ as the revelation itself and, hence, a concept like trinity is impossible. To them, Jesus remains just another prophet – albeit a very important one.[22]

Christians, on the other hand, have a hard time accepting that God revealed Himself once more and in a different manner. To them, the Qur'an remains just another book from a different religious tradition – though a bit of a problematic one.

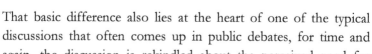

That basic difference also lies at the heart of one of the typical discussions that often comes up in public debates, for time and again, the discussion is rekindled about the perceived need for exegesis in the way Muslims deal with the Qur'an. Many contemporary Christians believe that Muslims do not want to engage with the historicity of the Qur'an. They thump themselves on the chest with their extensive library of academic exegesis, and act as if Muslims still live in the Middle Ages because they cling to the divinity of the Qur'an and because they refuse to see it as a human construct.

There is a huge fallacy in this reasoning, however. To believe that the Qur'an, at its core, is a divine revelation does not necessarily imply that Muslims would be incapable of engaging critically with the Qur'an. To realize how this can be so, ironically enough, we simply need to take a better look at Christian exegesis. Even though Christians still believe – as they have always done – that Christ is not only human but somehow also divine, it has not prevented the Christian tradition from engaging critically and historically with His life and words. Yet, however critical – and

---

[22] The specific place of Jesus within Islam is more thoroughly discussed in my conversation with Mona Siddiqui at the end of the book, p. 231 and onwards.

sometimes perhaps even hyper-critical – all sorts of scholars have been about 'the historical life' of Jesus, their research does not necessarily challenge the doctrine of trinity.

The same holds true for a Muslim view of the Qur'an. Even though the vast majority of Muslims has seen, still sees and always will see the Qur'an as a truly divine message, it does not prohibit them from understanding that revelation within its context, from searching for historic knowledge that broadens their view on certain passages or from distinguishing between verses that are more bound in time and space and verses that have a more universal character.

On top of it, exactly because the Prophet himself has always been seen as nothing but human, the Muslim tradition actually has a far longer history of critical engagement with the life of its founder, with the *hadith* collections a clear example.

The hadiths are the reports of the sayings and acts of the Prophet. Yet, because a tremendous amount of these stories and quotes abound, many scholars have worked extensively on determining which hadiths are authentic and which are not. To assess their authenticity, the scholars investigated their 'chains of narration'; that is to say, they researched the trustworthiness of the manner in which a certain hadith was passed from one person to another.

Nevertheless, no matter the amount of historic and scientific research Muslims engaged in and no matter the results, it did not abolish faith in revelation, for faith in revelation is simply something else. It's a belief that God can and does reveal himself in a manner that eventually eludes scientific research. It's a belief that human history can be penetrated by the divine.

Although such a faith or belief can often give rise to uncritical acceptance of problematic historical, theological or spiritual premises, it certainly doesn't do so by definition. In this respect, one can often hear Muslims refer to a hadith in which the Prophet said: "A Muslim should seek knowledge, even if he has to travel as far as China."[23]

In my case, it sufficed to go to London to find more knowledge about the language and the authority of the Qur'an. There I met Muhammad Abdel Haleem, a linguistics scholar who does not only know the Qur'an by heart, but also made one of the most brilliant English translations of the last decades.

---

[23] Although very popular among many Muslims, ironically enough, this particular hadith is probably not authentic. This doesn't matter all too much, however, since it's only a bit of a modern variation of an authentic and somewhat more general hadith in which the Prophet simply states: "Seeking knowledge is obligatory for every Muslim."

# MUHAMMAD ABDEL HALEEM
## ON THE LANGUAGE OF REVELATION

*When I met Cyrus McGoldrick, he told me that his favourite translation of the Qur'an was the one by Egyptian born Muhammad Abdel Haleem. I got a copy and quickly became just as impressed. One of the most remarkable aspects of the translation is the fact that it doesn't use any verse structure but is written as if it were fluent prose. In accordance with this stylistic choice, the language itself is free from the archaisms or awkward grammatical structures that are often found in other translations. As such, Abdel Haleem's translation excels in its transparent tone. Add to this the concise but tremendously interesting introduction and it becomes clear that it's by far the most accessible version for any contemporary English audience.*

*I met professor Haleem in his office at the London School of Oriental and African Studies, eager to know his views on the relationship between the text and context of the Qur'an.*

---------- ❀ ----------

In the Christian tradition, certainly today, the scriptures aren't seen as direct words of God but rather as works that are inspired by the Divine Spirit. It's a core element of the Islamic faith, however, that the Qur'an is a divine revelation. Yet, the Islamic tradition also recognizes the difference between 'revealed' and 'inspired' texts. So, how can we be

**certain that the Qur'an truly belongs to the first category?**

My colleagues in oriental departments might say that it was, in fact, Muhammad, or even others, who wrote the Qur'an. The theological tradition, on the other hand, maintains that he received it from an archangel who delivered it to him from God. But, as a scholar of linguistics, I deal with this only from the linguistic point of view, and I can see that what Muhammad received in the 'state of revelation' was very different from his normal language. We can see, for example, that the Qur'an is clearly of a higher level than the language of the hadith. We also know what Muhammad was capable of. We know that until his forties he didn't write any poetry and that he never gave speeches in public. It makes one wonder, therefore, how he, all of the sudden, could start to recite the verses of the Qur'an. The Muslims of the time said that the language came from God. The non-Muslims, however, said that he was a poet or that he had a *jinn*[24] who told him to say all the things he said. But whatever their explanation, they agreed on one thing: that the style of the Qur'an was much higher than the language people were used to. I have read the Qur'an for such a long time and I know it by heart but still, every day when I read the Qur'an, I discover new meanings in certain verses which I hadn't seen before. That's a special quality of the language of the Qur'an – even apart from the faith.

**And what about the structure and redaction of the Qur'an? In what measure were they influenced by people and context instead of divine revelation? The different revelations weren't put in chronological order, for example, and the *surahs*[25] are ordered longest to shortest. That implies quite some 'human'**

---

[24] A jinn is a supernatural being from Islamic mythology and theology. It's a sort of invisible spirit that can also take hold of human beings. The English word 'genie' is derived from this Arabic word.

[25] A surah is a chapter in the Qur'an.

**influence on the eventual Qur'an, does it not?**

I am convinced that there is a great unity in the material of every single surah. People often think it's a jumble of things, but it isn't. Through long studies of the 'linguistic habits' of the Qur'an, I can tell you that it is meticulously put together. The particular order of the surahs is a different story, however. Even Muslim scholars themselves have differing views on it. Some say the whole Qur'an is structured according to divine inspiration; others say that the specific arrangement of the surahs was the personal opinion of some of the Prophet's companions. These discussions have been going on for centuries.

**But if there might have been such an influence in the order of the surahs, why would we not go one step further and also suppose that, in the course of history, certain words might have changed or that some sentences might have been altered?**

I am convinced that the Qur'an, as we know it now, is exactly the same as the Prophet recited it and I base this conviction on several arguments.

First of all, we have to consider the length of Muhammad's prophethood. Jesus only had two and a half years to complete his mission, but Muhammad was there for twenty-three years. In the last ten years, he had thousands of companions and he was with them every day in the mosque, reciting the verses to them and making sure they had understood it correctly.

Second, in the Arab culture of those days, everything was learned by heart. Their genealogy, their history, their poetry, and so on, they memorized it all. And the Qur'an is only about five hundred pages. If we divide this over twenty-three years, two or three pages each month, then it becomes clear that it's really not beyond people's capacity to learn the Qur'an by heart.

Third, we have to keep in mind that people believed it was the word of God, because people who believe it's the word of God will exert great efforts in learning it properly. If you think how the first Muslims sacrificed themselves completely for the cause, it is difficult for me to imagine that they would deliberately change the words or concoct certain adaptations. That does not make sense. It makes a lot more sense to think that they would go to great lengths to retain the words exactly like the Prophet had told them.

On top of this, the Qur'an was put into writing on sundry materials during the lifetime of the Prophet. Only fourteen months after he died, a situation arose where everything had to be brought together and written down in one volume. Then, twenty years later, that first volume was copied and verified and six more copies were made. Nobody has ever dared to change anything in those texts. Even the orthography has retained peculiarities which no longer exist in Arabic writing but haven't been changed in the Qur'an.

Lastly, we shouldn't forget that the Qur'an, unlike all other scriptures, right from the beginning, was always protected by the heads of state. So, its integrity was always closely guarded by those in power.

As you notice, I don't use any theological arguments. When I teach, I don't use any theological arguments either, because my students aren't only Muslims. Sometimes they're Jewish, Christian, Hindu or Buddhist. I am not a theologian or a preacher; I am an academic and I deal with language, style and translation, so it's not my job to convince people of my faith.

**Did this consideration influence your translation as well?**

As you know, the Qur'an recognizes the scriptures sent to Moses and Jesus and acknowledges the prophets of these traditions. It says that all prophets came with the same message: to believe in one God and call people to act according to His law and it confirmed that they would have to account for their deeds on Judgement Day. That certainly affects my view. People often forget that the Qur'an calls upon Jews and Christians to stick to the teachings sent to them by God. So, as a Muslim, I would also like Christians to be very good Christians and Jews to be very good Jews. Some aren't, but I have also had the good fortune to meet some Christians that truly were living saints. I have met more Christians than Jews, but I'm certain there are saintly Jews as well. So, I don't condemn or judge people on the basis of their faith because I know from the Qur'an and the hadith that only God has the sole right to judge who goes to hell or paradise. No-one else can claim this right.

**Would you say that this premise makes your translation different from the others?**

Yes, but I only take this premise because it is a principle that the Qur'an itself expounds. Some people wrote to certain governments in the Arab world to say that my translation shouldn't be allowed because it was too lenient and liberal towards the Jews and the Christians. But I produced a very convincing counter argument from the Qur'an itself and it was accepted. They even bought a large amount of copies for distribution. *(Muhammad laughs.)*

**One of the verses which I find quite exemplary for the somewhat 'softer tone' of your translation is 14:4. In most translations, I read: "God leads astray whoever He will and guides whoever He will." But you translate the verse as: "God leaves whoever He will to stray, and guides whoever He will." That seemed a small but important difference to me for it implies a lot more choice and less determinism.**

In my translations, I always keep in mind what the Qur'an says in other passages. In this case, we have to refer to the beginning of chapter 2, verse 26, where it is said that God leads astray only those who already choose to be astray. On top of this, linguistically speaking, this particular form of the verb can also be translated in the sense of: "He finds them misguided or astray." So, yes, it's less direct than is often translated.

**Another part of your translation that struck me was the way you translated *Al-Fatiha*.[26] Your translation reads: "In the name of God, the Lord of Mercy, the Giver of Mercy! Praise belongs to God, Lord of the Worlds, the Lord of Mercy, the Giver of Mercy, Master of the Day of Judgement. It is You we worship; it is You we ask for help. Guide us to the straight path: the path of those You have blessed, those who incur no anger and who have not gone astray." I was especially surprised by your choice of the expression 'those who incur no anger'. Most translations state something like 'those who have evoked Your anger'. In a footnote, you also add: "Note that the word 'anger' is not attributed to God, as it is in many translations." Again, a small but very significant change.**

I can bet anyone a million dollars that I'm not mistaken, because it is as clear as a summer sun in the Middle East that my translation concurs with the original Arabic Qur'an. But previous translators have always written what was written by others before them, without looking at what was really there in the Arabic. God isn't mentioned. It doesn't say that God is angry with them. It might say 'God is angry' somewhere else in the Qur'an, but not in the Fatiha. The important thing is that God is presented as loving, compassionate, merciful and guiding. So, the old translations jar with the main picture which is presented in Al-Fatiha.

---

[26] Al-Fatiha is the opening chapter of the Qur'an. The translation quoted is taken from M.A.S. Abdel Haleem, *The Qur'an. A new translation*, Oxford University Press, 2004.

**I would guess that it sometimes seems almost impossible to find the proper translation for certain words and sentences since, as this example shows, translation often also implies interpretation.**

The arrangement of the words in the Qur'an, indeed, brings a richness of meaning which you can't possibly bring into the English, because the same statement in Arabic can have three or four different meanings which are all relevant. So, after you have done everything you could to translate it as properly as possible, you're still disappointed. English simply doesn't have the same words with such a multiplicity of meanings and you end up selecting only one layer of meaning. An Egyptian scholar from Oxford called me up one day and asked about the translation I made of a particular verse. After I told her, she said: "The Arabic is so much better." But I replied to her: "Listen, I never claimed to be as eloquent as the author." *(Muhammad laughs)*

# SHARIA

Contrary to what many people think, the *sharia* is not a set of legal codes written down clearly in the Qur'an or some other book. As a concept, it above all refers to the divine law that undergirds life and the moral code that flows from it. Throughout history, however, the exact nature and content of the sharia has remained a never ending matter of interpretation and debate. That's where *fiqh* comes in since fiqh is the theological and juridical 'practice' that tries to unravel this law of the divine and its moral code. In other words, fiqh is the search for the proper and practical implementation of the sharia within daily life. And just like our present day juridical systems, the Islamic 'juridotheology' of sharia and fiqh has always been discussed and re-discussed among different scholars, fractions, orders and schools.

However, people who don't have an Islamic background are mostly unaware of the wide variety of ideological branches in the Islamic world. They see Islam as a homogenous block that follows one distinct body of rules and regulations, while in reality, Islam is a hugely decentralized religion with an enormous diversity in cultural and spiritual practices.

If we, thus, would like to make a comparison between the structures of Christianity and Islam, we should liken Islam to the Protestant world and contrast it with the Roman Catholic Church. Because within Islam, there is no obvious centre of authority, such as the Pope, and there is no single canon of laws.

It is, therefore, insufficient to be aware of the typical encyclopaedic divisions in order to properly grasp the multiplicity of authority within Islam. It's not enough, for example, to know that there is a difference between *Sunni* and *Shia*[27] or to know that there are four different juridical schools within Sunni Islam.

When we delve deeper into Sunni Islam, for example, we will quickly come to realise that there aren't any 'heads' of those different juridical schools, but that they are merely schools of thought that have once laid down certain fundamental principles of dealing with Islam. And out of those schools of thought grew an enormous number of different groups, movements and orders.

The diversity within Shia Islam is just as big. Even though many Shia groups will adhere to the idea of a spiritual (and often also worldly) head who should lead their community, by now, the Shia have split into such a large number of different factions that it might take many years to get to know and understand them all.

This enormous spiritual, theological and ideological variety is only amplified by the specific histories of certain regions, countries and states since Islam has always strongly 'encultured' itself wherever it spread. Moroccan Muslims will uphold many particular traditions that Turkish Muslims don't, the state ideology of Saudi Arabia

---

[27] Sunni and Shia are the two main denominations of Islam. Sunni's comprise about 85 to 90 per cent of Muslims worldwide. The 10 to 15 per cent of Shia Muslims can be predominantly found in Iran and Iraq, and within large minority communities in Afghanistan, Pakistan, Yemen, Bahrain, Syria, and Lebanon. The original split between Sunni and Shia was above all a political disagreement about the succession of the leadership of the early Muslim community. After the death of the Prophet, he was succeeded by the four rightly guided caliphs (Abu Bakr, Umar, Uthman ibn Affan and Ali). When Ali, the nephew and son-in-law of the Prophet, became caliph, certain groups revolted against him. Those that supported Ali and who thought that the following caliphs should belong to Ali's lineage became the Shia. After Ali was murdered, however, Muawiyah became the next caliph and those who kept on following the caliph became the Sunni. Throughout the centuries, certain doctrinal and ritual differences have arisen, such as the emphasis on reverence for Ali in Shia Islam or the division in different 'schools of law' in Sunni Islam.

starkly contrasts with the look and feel of Islam in China, and so on.

This is not to say that one cannot understand anything of Islam without an elaborate and exhaustive overview of all the different branches. Few, if any, Muslims actually have such an overview themselves. But in order to get a bit of a grasp, it is at least essential to realise that, despite the sectarian tensions some subgroups might create, the unity of Islam eventually exists in its fundamental acceptance of its diversity. The best example thereof is probably the yearly hajj that brings together millions of Muslim pilgrims from different denominations and from all over the world as they whirl around the Kaaba.

In a sense, perhaps, the only thing that truly binds the Ummah, the Muslim community, is the direction of their prayer towards the Kaaba in Mecca and the shahada, the Islamic 'act of faith' which, as was explained earlier, states that there is no God but God and that Muhammad is one of his prophets. But apart from such very basic elements, the expressions of sharia are just as diverse as the cultural differences between the various Muslim communities.

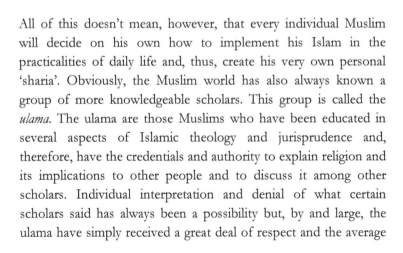

All of this doesn't mean, however, that every individual Muslim will decide on his own how to implement his Islam in the practicalities of daily life and, thus, create his very own personal 'sharia'. Obviously, the Muslim world has also always known a group of more knowledgeable scholars. This group is called the *ulama*. The ulama are those Muslims who have been educated in several aspects of Islamic theology and jurisprudence and, therefore, have the credentials and authority to explain religion and its implications to other people and to discuss it among other scholars. Individual interpretation and denial of what certain scholars said has always been a possibility but, by and large, the ulama have simply received a great deal of respect and the average

Muslim would turn to them for advice.

On the other hand, many Muslims also speak of a crisis within the present day ulama. In this respect, there is no need to deny that the traditional mode of debate and discussion has often been replaced by strict teachings that leave no room for dissent or personal interpretation. As such, we are sometimes confronted with surprising examples of scholars and groups that proclaim a sharia full of sometimes mind-bogglingly silly *fatwas*.[28]

So where does that leave us today? What do we make of all of this? What are the precise evolutions? Who carries authority within the contemporary Ummah and to what extent?

In order to get a clearer picture on these matters, I visited Shaykh Abdal Hakim Murad, acknowledged by many as one of the most influential people within the present day ulama.

---

[28] The word fatwa is often misunderstood. It is not a religious dogma that binds every Muslim all over the world. A fatwa is merely a juridical/theological 'advice' or 'council' of a certain scholar. When scholars are confronted with a question about the correct conduct in certain situations, they formulate their stance on the matter and base this stance on their interpretation of sharia, hadith and the Qur'an. This stance and the argumentation leading up to it is a fatwa. Traditionally, fatwas were, therefore, only presented after thorough debate between different scholars and after solid research of the scriptural sources. Thus, one scholar's fatwa can easily deny the fatwa of another.

# ABDAL HAKIM MURAD
# ON AUTHORITY WITHIN ISLAM

*Few people in the Islamic world bridge East and West, tradition and modernity like Abdal Hakim Murad. He studied and lectured at both Cambridge and Al-Azhar,[29] but also sat at the feet of Sufi shaykhs and gives regular spiritual lectures in his local mosque. He's on the board of The Research Center for Islamic Legislation and Ethics in Doha, but he also holds the position of Dean at the Cambridge Muslim College. He translated important classical works, but he's also a regular contributor in the British media. From the start of our meeting, however, I was above all struck by the way he combined vast knowledge and intellectual sharpness with straightforward humbleness.*

*Because of his experiences and expertise, I specifically wanted to talk to Shaykh Abdal Hakim Murad about the evolutions of authority within the global Ummah. As the old 'centres of authority' are either non-existent or lost the impact they once had, I hoped to learn from him which institutions or individuals are gradually becoming new points of reference. It became one of the most enlightening conversations of my life.*

———— ❀ ————

---

[29] Al-Azhar is an important Egyptian University in Cairo. It was founded around 970 AD and is, therefore, one of the very first universities in the world. Until today it's one of the most important academic strongholds in the Muslim world.

**It is often claimed Islam has no institutionalized authority, but if we honestly look at history, we can see that there have, in fact, always been certain 'centres of authority'. The first caliphs, the Al-Azhar University, the scholars of Damascus, the Ottoman Sultan . . . they have all been examples of concentrated authority. Today, however, it seems very difficult to find such centres or to assess the authority of the many different groups, institutions and individuals. Would you say, then, that today's situation is an anomaly in the history of Islam?**

If you have a religion with ethics, that religion will want its ethics reflected in the laws and, of course, you can't have a legal system or courts without having some structural authority. Yet, in the early centuries, Islamic law was as decentred as it could possibly be. Each *khadi*[30] was de facto independent and there was no statutory legislation.

In the nineteenth century, however, the Ottomans had to reshape Islamic law into statutory law, because in order to create a stable trading environment for their European partners, they needed certain treaties and regulations. That led to the establishment of a juridical code called the *'Mecelle'*.

Nowadays, many Muslims assume that Islamic law has always been statutory but, in fact, it's a kind of 'Westernization'. In the age before the state got involved with legislation it was something that grew from the ground up. Even more so, originally, the ulama represented the Muslims *against* the deprivations of the state.

So historically, despite the oversimplifications, the structure of the religion and its authority have been detached from the structure and authority of the state. People often tend to think that in Islam, religion and politics are the same, while, in fact, there was probably a closer interlocking between religion and the state in many

---

[30] A khadi is a Muslim judge.

Christian states than in many Islamic parts of the world. In the traditional Catholic world, often the empire and the church were one institution, while the Islamic society knew the strange situation in which the scholars weren't a part of the imperial bureaucracy. But once statutory law became the norm worldwide, it was impossible for the scholars to remain independent. If the state started to legislate – which it wasn't supposed to do in Islamic law – either they could take the stance that the state just legislates on the basis of its own secular pragmatism or they could try to 'reduce the damage' by becoming state employees. That led to concepts like 'the grand *mufti*'[31] of a certain country or 'the Islamic university' of a certain state.

Nowadays, therefore, the ulama are often integrated into the state's mechanisms. They have a hard job not becoming the state's representatives, putting forward only those fatwas that the state approves. They've become a kind of 'clerisy' and are often seen as a part of a hypocritical bureaucracy. Hence, the crisis of authority the 'establishment ulama' finds itself in.

**How, then, does this crisis of authority express itself in the contemporary Islamic world?**

The situation the traditional ulama sees us as being in at the moment is a kind of 'emergency mode'. In traditional sharia terminology, such a time of emergency is called '*nawazil*'. That's the category you apply when there is a huge political misfortune, such as the expulsion of the Muslims in the Iberian Peninsula by the Spanish Inquisition. All kinds of new rulings come into place in such a period because if you followed the classical fiqh, you'd be killed. And since the models of many of our present societies are alien to the premises on which the traditional sharia rests, we are considered to be in such a nawazil period. For example, the

---

[31] A mufti is an Islamic scholar who is an interpreter of sharia and, thus, an expounder of fiqh.

traditional sharia assumes the existence of the extended family. So, when the wife is divorced, the husband wasn't supposed to continually support her because others would take care of her. Nowadays, however, we get into situations where some people wouldn't be looked after or cared for. So, what do you do when the basic assumptions that underlie the regulations aren't prevalent anymore?

The fall of the *caliphate*[32] was another reason for considering the situation of emergency. Until the 1920s, less than a hundred years ago, every Sunni Muslim in the world had some dim idea that behind the diversity of Islam, there was ultimately a unifying principle: the Sultan and the Shaykh al-Islam of the Ottoman ulama. If you had a dispute in Sunni Islam over doctrine or sharia, theoretically, there was someone who could resolve it. It wasn't binding, but it was authoritative because it came from the Shaykh al-Islam. This was eventually abolished by Atatürk and nothing has really stepped in to replace that.

In a way, the abolition of the caliphate certainly proved that the decentred nature of sharia most certainly remains a strength because destroying one part didn't do much to the organism as a whole. So, the destruction of the caliphate certainly didn't destroy Islam. Nonetheless, after a while, the unity of the community on the sensitive nawazil related issues becomes very doubtful and certain people started to base their fatwas too much on their immediate political circumstances or their psychological state. On the basis of the basic justification of nawazil fiqh – which is 'to do what keeps you alive' – they let slip the precision instruments of the classical Islamic jurisprudence. As such, they came up with

[32] A caliphate is an Islamic sovereign polity led by a caliph. The successions of Muslim empires that have existed in the Muslim world are, therefore, usually described as caliphates. The Ottoman Empire was the last caliphate and was abolished by Atatürk in 1924. The caliphate that was proclaimed by Abu Bakr al-Baghdadi in 2014 wasn't recognized by the great majority of Muslims and, as such, cannot be properly considered a real caliphate.

things like suicide bombing, which is completely inconceivable in traditional Islamic sensibilities. We're not even supposed to tattoo our bodies because it is sacrosanct, so forget about killing ourselves. But the idea of the Palestinians, for example, is that there is no caliph, that nobody in the world is going to help and that the injustices continue so that they can only reach for things that would normally not be justifiable. They see it as the only option instead of just letting the Israelis sit on their head forever.

**So, in the absence of authority, we see pragmatism winning over morality?**

Fundamentalism often coalesces with pragmatism because they do not see themselves bound by the tradition or the restraint ethos of that tradition. They're thrown back on the scripture and their own psychic state and don't consider the consensus of hundreds of years of cautious scholars. So, the angry man alone in a room with a scripture is, in a sense, more powerful than the scripture on its own. For the scripture in itself is quite tender, passive and vulnerable and can be twisted into serving any purpose – which is increasingly what we're seeing.

If we look at the famous fatwa of Bin Laden against Jews and Crusaders, for instance, which authorizes every Muslim to kill any American combatant or non-combatant, it is phrased in a way that indicates that he had no idea what a traditional fatwa looks like. He doesn't refer to any of the classical debates, to any of his predecessors or any consultation of the chain of narration. He just said: "They're attacking us so we have to defend ourselves." Then he quoted a Qur'anic verse that says we're, indeed, allowed to defend ourselves, and from it deducted that we can, therefore, kill Americans.

It is baseless in terms of traditional Islamic argumentation, but all he had to do to spread his idea was to throw his fatwa on the Internet. This is something the traditional scholarship can't really cope with because that scholarship is so non-hierarchical.

## Do you think this situation will change?

As soon as things settle down and people stop panicking, as soon as the drones stop buzzing over our heads, it will become evident to the majority of the Muslims that hot-headed efforts of the narrowest interpretations don't actually work in practice. It's a messy thing that hasn't really 'delivered' anywhere. Iran was the first place where it had a chance to prove itself, but Iran is one of the most secular places around when you look at the daily lives of people.[33]

The wiser heads will say that there is much to be gained from reconnecting to tradition and traditional scholarship. In some cases, however, it's not really accessible. In Libya, for example, Gaddafi killed it off for forty years. There were some old scholars there, but reconnecting teenagers is really difficult for people in their seventies and eighties.

However, one of the huge advantages of the non-clerical model which Islam favours is that you're not stuck when your local spiritual leader is completely uncongenial. You can simply go to another mosque. And I think part of the resilience of today's Islam lies in the fact that they can go down the road to a different mosque and find someone else who does deal with their issues. The danger is, of course, that they might be following voices that pander to their insecurities rather than reassuring them that God is still in control of history.

## Would you say then, like some do, that the crisis of authority leads to a crisis of Islam as a whole?

---

[33] Mosque attendance, for example, is very low in Iran. It's one of those facts that easily surprises people, but the percentage of people who goes to the mosque on a weekly basis in Iran is one of the lowest in the Muslim world. Friday prayers and sermons are attended by very few people.

The merit of the decentred model is to be seen in the fact that in spite of the talk of 'the crisis of Islam' or 'what went wrong with Islam', many mosques are still crowded until overflowing. Despite the decrepitude of the structures, the collapse of traditional Islamic education in many places, people still want Islam, even in those places that the West had declared secular.

I think it actually makes many people in the West feel a bit uneasy. Sociologists said it was impossible since 'liberated' people were supposed to want secularism. Yet, even though the Tunisian government for fifty years deliberately tried to squeeze religion out of the Tunisian soul, as soon as they get the chance, they vote for whoever has the longest beard or quotes the Qur'an. And we can give more examples. In a country like Turkey, which was very strong in promoting secularism, mosques are still full. In Europe as well, Muslim minorities are still pretty resistant to many secularizing tendencies.

We have even come to the point where it becomes difficult to claim that Christianity is still the default religion. There are churches everywhere, but there is nothing much going on inside them. Many people are either in the shopping malls or in the mosques.

I, therefore, don't accept there is a crisis of Islam. Actually, I think Islam is the great religious success story of modernity . . . despite itself. Ultimately, you judge a religion and the validity of its truth claims on the basis of whether it is still appealing to people or not. And people keep converting to Islam.

The Islamic leadership, however, isn't ready at all to assume that position. Their discourse, theology or vision of history isn't prepared for it. They are still in their nawazil mode of 'what's the latest headline and how do we panic next?' The cartoons, Israel, terror . . . it's all boiling, but the reality on the ground is that something *is* in fact working.

**You say Islam is the big success story of modernity but, at**

the same time, the debates which bring everything to the 'boiling point' are often about the friction between certain tenets of modernity – like secularism – and the way Islam tries to position itself within society.

Much, indeed, depends on how the Western world will respond to the unexpected collapse of the default religion. Not so much in the US but certainly in Europe, because in Europe, the sense is now that the host society is not *ahl al-kitab*.[34] That is to say, the people in Europe aren't seen any longer as 'people of the book', Christian or Jewish, but just as hedonistic. That makes it harder to continue the discourse in traditional Islamic categories. It also makes the conversation generally more difficult because very often secularity finds it very hard to develop a language to deal with religious people. The Catholic Church finds ways of talking to Muslims – sometimes it gets it wrong, but there's common ground there – but it's really hard to converse with this sort of 'Darwinian fundamentalism' of the belief in the selfish gene.

It may well be that, as with the Jewish marginalization, this will secure the distinctiveness and survival of the Muslim communities. A benign neglect would quite quickly bring about assimilation, but a sense that the mainstream doesn't like certain people makes it easier for those people to retreat in their own values. They wonder why they should integrate into a society that doesn't like them.

I have the feeling that many of the young people who find themselves right in the middle of the debates on identity, culture, religion and society don't go to the traditional ulama, their mosques or the institutions of their community for

---

[34] The term 'ahl al-kitab', which is literally translated as 'people of the book', designates non-Muslim adherents to faiths which have a revealed scripture. The Qur'an mentions Jews, Sabians and Christians as three types of adherents, though it does not say these are the only ones. The concept should, therefore, not by definition be limited to these three.

**advice. Instead they seem to turn to inspirational speakers
like Tariq Ramadan, Amr Khaled, Hamza Yussuf, Zakir
Naiq and many others who often draw big crowds. I'm not
trying to assess their specific teachings or personalities here,
but could it be said, in general, that such people are
becoming somewhat new authoritative figures?**

I don't know. The penetration of their substantive ideas in the
normative Muslim communities is very hard to map. It's hard to
see out there that there are mosques that 'follow' them or that
there are organizations, websites and magazines that step in their
line.

If you look at the younger generation in the UK, most of them still
associate themselves with the traditional scholars of the
subcontinent. They're fiercely loyal. The number of Muslims who
can detach themselves from their own religious upbringing and
who are interested in something different with a more international
character is probably very small – in the UK, perhaps forty to fifty
thousand all together. Some of them might attach themselves to
certain charismatic speakers, and those speakers can become big
stars, so to speak, but there are also others who think the solution
is a *Salafi*[35] alternative, which has the advantages of being well
funded and of having a strong presence on the Internet. And the
Salafis can, of course, do what they like because of the close ties
the British government has with Saudi Arabia.

**Is there a bit of a gap, then, between the traditional**

---

[35] Salafism is a particular movement within Islam that strictly focusses on the first
sources of Islam. Therefore, its practices are based solely on the Qur'an and the
example of the Prophet and his companions. In fact, the term 'salafi' takes its
name from the word 'salaf', which means 'predecessors' or 'ancestors' and is used
to identify the earliest Muslims. Salafis, thus, try to conform as much as possible
to the life of those earliest Muslims. Yet, in itself, the Salafi movement is a very
modern and reactionary movement that denounces many other aspects of the
Islamic tradition that were built up during the centuries as unlawful innovations.

**scholarship and the 'inspirational speakers' or the leaders of certain movements? And shouldn't that gap somehow be bridged?**

There are many facets to it. A. We live in a time where everything is changing fast. B. Many scholars aren't subsidized like they used to be in the past. C. The responsibilities to master the traditional mechanisms of Islamic law require an immense amount of memorization, patience and wisdom. D. They need to meaningfully understand the modern world and the place of the religious community within it. As such, it is extremely difficult for young Muslims to master all of this.

So, the scholarship becomes a bit divided between scholars who are westernized but don't know the sharia as they should, and traditional scholars who are often very cautious about expressing any views at all about modernity.

**When I came to you, I had somehow hoped to find out more about where the new 'centres of authority' could be found in contemporary Islam. Yet, I have the feeling that you think it's all quite uncertain, that they are everywhere and nowhere at the moment.**

Religion, as you know, is very hard to predict. So, when anybody asks: "Where is it going?" I would have to answer: "God only knows." The current situation would have been unguessable twenty years ago.

**And where do you place yourself in all of it?**

I'm simply an academic of Cambridge and I try my best to be involved in various projects on the local as well as the international level, but it would surprise me that many Muslims in the UK have ever heard of me. I guess they know my brother, Henry Winter, a lot better since he's a famous sports journalist.

**Quite a modest answer, considering your standing among the international ulama.[36] Your position might even surprise certain people since you're an English convert who places himself within the Sufi tradition. Yet, you're not the first highly respected scholar I spoke to whose teachers have been Sufis so, by now, I've come to the conclusion that Sufism isn't at all such a 'marginalized' aspect of Islam as people often claim.**

That's true. If you look at the Ottoman Empire, for example, nobody ever was 'against' Sufism. This concept of Islam being anti-Sufi is there because of Saudi puritanism, but that's a very recent evolution. And even Saudi Arabia is full of Sufis. In Medina, I went to some of the biggest Sufi gatherings you can imagine.

Above all, it's important to remember that it's not so much about Sufism itself. Sufism is just a name. The ultimate proof of the religion is the saints. They are the miraculous expressions of divine love, and it's through them that we come to know the Prophet.

The Prophet isn't just the theory. He has always been a living part of Islam. He was a fully realized, fully alert, God-send human being who was at the centre of his society and miraculously transformed that society. And after he died, he became the living heart of Muslim piety and most certainly the centre of Sufism. That takes people some time to learn, because in the West, they often see Islam as a regression to some 'Moses-style' religion, but that whole letter-spirit dichotomy doesn't make sense to us. Of course we need letters, because we need boundaries in our lives, we need rules and we need rituals, but there has to be spirit as well. And that spirit is what the Prophet *is*. He is the sharia, the ethical

---

[36] Abdal Hakim Murad has consistently been included in the "500 Most Influential Muslims" list published by the Royal Islamic Strategic Studies Centre of Jordan. In 2012, he was ranked the 50th most influential.

boundaries, but also the *mi'raj*, the spiritual ascension.

The saint in Islam is, therefore, the one who shows you the greatness of the Prophet because his life meticulously conforms to the last detail of the *sunnah*[37] out of total love and surrender. The self is gone and only the Prophetic form remains. The dignity, the ancient wisdom, the selflessness, the love for others . . . you see it in the Prophet and you see it in the saint.

**Did you meet many people who you would call saints like that?**

Sure, but they don't always show up the way you'd want it. Sometimes they're very scary. Sometimes they beat you up because that's what you need and deserve. They take a stick and hit you until the rubbish comes out.

The Western seeker has this mystical 'George Harrison idea' of a white-haired sage in a cabin in the Himalayas who gives you a bit of advice that makes you feel really spiritual and enlightened. But that's not the reality of it. The reality is a lot of fasting, tears, shedding blood, being hit . . . The function of the teacher is to beat you. The word 'guru' in Sanskrit actually means 'heavy', but many seekers do not want that. They want light and smooth spirituality with nice incense and chanting. True saints, however, sometimes tell you all about yourself. You see them two minutes a year and they can tell you: "You've done this and that while you should do that and this." They leave you flabbergasted as to how they knew; you go away and you're completely shattered and ruined, but it does help you spiritually advance. And then they go on and help another thousand people.

**What do you think is the reason that they are so capable of**

---

[37] The 'lifestyle' of the Muslim. Literally it means 'tradition'. It is the Islamic way of life prescribed as normative for Muslims on the basis of the Prophet's example in the way he spoke, acted and behaved.

**helping people to spiritually advance?**

The saints remind us of the fact that religion is not about doing stuff for the sake of treats after death, but that it's about consciousness and remembrance now and in every moment. They remind us that it's about constantly being *in* God. In the saints you see the royal qualities and incredible dignity that such a consciousness brings about. Just being with them makes you kind of reconfigure yourself completely.

So, when you see them, you discover what love is really all about. Our culture sings about love endlessly because it actually doesn't have any of it. It became the basis of our society but it's a kind of coitus interruptus: the slogan of 'love is all you need' is everywhere on the covers of magazines, in music and soap operas, but it's not really there. People need it, they have the yearning, but nothing is giving it to them so they're sort of endlessly trying new things. I see it with my students as well. Their girlfriends dump them and they try again and again . . . but, basically, you can love anybody. If you're not so fussy about it, you can marry anybody as long as you let God constrain you on the rubbish.

A saint is beyond that sort of narrow-minded egocentrism and shows us what real divine love is about.

**Could I conclude, then, that the true spiritual authorities in Islam, according to you, are the saints?**

Like I often say: "If you have not seen the saint, you have not seen the sunnah."

# SUFIYA

Throughout the history of Islam, theology and jurisprudence have been intertwined to a far greater extent than they have been in the Christian world. In Christian eyes, this might often seem to lead to strange 'hair splitting' discussions about what is *halal* (proper) and what is *haram* (forbidden).[38] Thus, it can seem very out of place in this day and age when scholars and individuals discuss whether listening to pop music is allowed or whether one can eat shellfish. On the other hand, Christians can be very charmed when they come across the poetry and the mysticism of the *Sufiya*.[39] Regardless of their particular religious background, many spiritual

---

[38] Most people know the term halal in relation to food; for example, because of the fact that animals have to be slaughtered in a ritual way before Muslims can consider them to be halal. But halal and its counterpart, haram, can be applied to almost any act or product. When the fiqh has determined that certain deeds or the use of certain products are in accordance with the sharia, they are considered to be proper and lawful and, thus, halal. And when, on the other hand, the fiqh has determined that certain deeds or the use of certain products transgress the sharia, scholars will deem them haram and Muslims should, therefore, refrain from them.

[39] Sufiya is the plural of Sufi. The word is used here to refer to the many great mystic saints Islam has known. It is, thus, distinguished from the more commonly used English plural 'Sufis', which simply means 'adherents of Sufism'. For it's not because people are somehow connected to certain mystical traditions that they are also highly evolved spiritual people. In fact, the Arabic language makes a distinction between Sufi and *mutasawwif*. The mutasawwif is someone who is still trying to walk the mystical path, while the Sufi is someone who is 'at the end' of the path.

seekers find much depth in their poetry of ego-transcendence, love and unity.

I had always been very drawn to such mystics and poets myself. Even more so, in my own life as well, they were my initial door into Islam. Yet, through my Halal Monk journey, it gradually became clear to me that, nowadays, we hold a rather distorted view of Sufism. In my conversations with Feisal Abdul Rauf, Peter Sanders and Abdal Hakim Murad, I had already briefly touched upon the subject and, thus, became aware of my misconceptions. One of the biggest misconceptions, for example, is to view 'Sufism' as some 'different side', as something which is detached from mainstream Islam. The truth of the matter is that it's actually an essential and integral part of it.

Mysticism, theology and jurisprudence form an intricate whole in Islam, and Christians sometimes have a hard time understanding how this can be so since concepts like mysticism and sharia seem light years apart in the eyes of Westerners and contemporary Christians. But this is not the case in the Islamic world. In the Islamic world, we can find an enormous amount of theological discussion on rules and regulations of human conduct, as well as an enormous amount of mystical poetry and spiritual music. And it's not like one is the mainstream and the other is the margin. They are both aspects of the same whole. Classical textbooks can, thus, describe juridical matters on one page, then talk about cosmological principles on the following page, and finally conclude the chapter with a mystical poem.

———————— ❁ ————————

Like Abdal Hakim Murad explained, Westerners often see Islam as some sort of "regression to a 'Moses-style' religion", although the dichotomy between letter and spirit simply makes less sense within Islam. The spirit is to be found within the letter and vice versa. That is why he stated that the true authority eventually resides with the saints who meticulously combine the two.

The 13th century Mevlana Rumi was one of those Sufi saints. His works are still very popular today, also among Westerners. Yet, many people tend to perceive him as some sort of 'free floating' artist or poet and forget (or ignore) that he had a very firm grasp of what Islamic theology and jurisprudence are all about because of his classical education.

Rumi is also the founder of the Mevlevi order. The members of that order are commonly known as the 'whirling dervish', who wear wide robes and a brown fez on their heads while they whirl around their axis during a trance like musical ritual called the *sema*. This sema is an effort to go to the very essence of one's soul and, in so doing, find unity with the divine. As such, this sema is also an example of the spiritual heart of Islam.

This impressive ritual appeals to many Westerners as well. That's not surprising at all considering the gracious circular movements of the dance and the soft melodies of the trance music. They aren't aware, however, that such mystical and spiritual aspects of Islam are also often abused nowadays for commercial and political purposes. This became quite clear to me during my conversation with Kudsi Ergüner.

*Photo by Wijnand Schouten*

# KUDSI ERGÜNER
## ON THE SPIRITUAL DEPTH OF ISLAM

*Kudsi Ergüner is a contemporary master of classical Ottoman Sufi music. From an early age, his father taught him to play the ney, the reed flute which is ever present in Turkish Sufi music. It was the time when the young Turkish secular republic wanted to break with its religious past, deemed the old traditional Sufi rituals forbidden and disbanded the Mevlevi order. However, because Kudsi belonged to the Ergüner family, he had the good fortune to be surrounded by the last people who held the key to this Sufi tradition. Away from the supervision of the state, they secretly held their rituals in small places in Istanbul.*

———— ❁ ————

**These days, Sufism and Mevlana Rumi are all around in Turkey, from little dolls in tourist shops to big discussions on talk shows. I guess that's quite different compared to the time when you grew up in Istanbul.**

Looking back, it was a very interesting period because we formed a bridge between the old traditions and the present day, when different religious organisations are once again allowed. But nowadays, Sufism is much exploited politically – not only in Turkey but worldwide. In the supposed conflict between the secular West and the Muslim world, Sufism is presented as the 'modern', 'light' or 'open' version of Islam. Yet, Sufism is pure Islam just like any other form of Islam. So, you can't try to solve the problem between the West and Islam – which I actually think is more a problem of modernity, capitalism and geo-politics than of religion – by acting as if Sufism is less 'strictly' religious. There is no Sufism without Islam and there is no Islam without Sufism. Today, however, people want to create a new sort of Sufism, which relates more to commercialized spirituality and New Age.

Real Sufism is a sort of 'self-education'. The human being is in between being an animal and a human being, and in Sufism, it is believed that the real reason for our creation is 'to become human'. The context of the Sufi *tariqas*[40] is, therefore, to help people find this necessary education and elevation. Yet, many people who supposedly talk of Sufism don't refer to this inner work. They only say, 'oh, we love each other', 'oh, we are so tolerant', and so on. But for me, this is a 'Catholic' version of Islam. Of course 'love' is the main topic of tasawwuf. But the love that the Sufiya of old generations were talking about is not the same love that those people speak of. The love of the Sufiya is a love for God that brings us beyond the ego.

**Is your music a way for you 'to become human'? Do you see it as a tool to 'transcend' your 'animal self'?**

We can't give a reason for everything we do. Of course, some people explain their acts with big words, but I'm not like that. I'm a musician and I love music. That's it.

I am, of course, convinced that the early Sufis were deeply affected by the music they made. It was not just some frivolous enjoyment but a deep experience. Today, it is very rare for people to have such a deep feeling and deep understanding of the music, but the

---

[40] A tariqa is a school, brotherhood or order. Therefore, in the context of Sufism, it refers to a spiritual community lead by a shaykh whose teachings are in accordance with the teachings of the founder of the tariqa.

repertoire is there and it's a beautiful repertoire. So why wouldn't we play it, without any pretention?

**As a musician you also seem to have a great interest in mixing your music with the music of other cultures, like the way you fused it with jazz or French renaissance music. Isn't it sometimes very difficult to fuse different sets of musical systems?**

If you remain sincere with yourself, if you have something to say through your music, and if you don't mindlessly imitate others, then there doesn't have to be any problem at all. Yet, I think this is a philosophical problem that does not only apply to music and which is of particular importance today. Can one person live in the UK, Belgium or France, but still remain Turkish? In Europe, more and more, people want you to assimilate. So we have to ask ourselves: What makes me myself? What do I need to retain to remain myself? That means you have to eliminate certain unnecessary things that aren't very important and keep other more essential things. It's the same in music. For example, we can't leave our intervals. Each *maqam*, that is to say, each melodic phrase has specific intervals, but if I give them up to go easier with the European intervals, I lose myself. In none of my albums, therefore, do I abandon those intervals.

When I left Turkey in the seventies it was a bit like the Soviet bloc. The country was very closed up and constantly trying to protect itself from other countries. But after the eighties, it wasn't possible anymore, neither economically nor culturally. So, what happens is that the dominant culture of the world, which, right now, is the Western commercial culture, invades countries like Turkey. That is why I believe artists have a duty to underline the differences, to insist on particularity and, in so doing, protect our identities from this invasion of commercial 'mass culture'. I take that duty upon myself as well, because I want to say to people that, if we want a new global culture, we need to respect others *and* ourselves.

**That brings us back to the contemporary interest in Sufism, for can't the teachings of the Sufiya be of much help in this matter? Don't they contain a lot of elements that oppose such a consumption culture?**

Most certainly, but sadly enough, that's not what we're talking about when we speak of Sufism these days.

Some claim they know something about Sufism simply because their grandfathers were Sufiya. Others claim they're 'masters' and that they have special powers which can cure people. But neither of those groups teaches the real tradition of Sufism. They only tell their own theories and ideas.

Still others refer to Turkish tradition to claim their authority in the Muslim world. However, in Turkey, there has been at least fifty years of 'nothingness' during which the tradition wasn't continued, so such references are simply false.

**You refer to the fact that the line of the Mevlevis had been cut so that the tariqa, in fact, doesn't exist anymore. How does that make you feel about the Mevlevi Ensemble of Konya that tours around the world?**

That ensemble is nothing more than a group of people who work in the Folklore Department of the Ministry of Culture. So, it's more a matter of tourism than tradition, although they act as if the people in the show are real dervishes.

In the seventies, I toured around the world with my father to give the first presentations of sema, the ceremony of the whirling dervishes. We were honest about what we did. We simply wanted to show the tradition and let people know that it was forbidden in Turkey. But then, all of the sudden, the Turkish government took it over. They didn't do it to tell about the tradition. They used it to

THE SPIRITUAL DEPTH OF ISLAM

sell their country.

**And what is your opinion on those DJs and musicians who try to explicitly mix the traditional with the modern by mixing club beats with Sufi elements?**

The problem is that when you say 'Sufi elements', in fact, those aren't 'Sufi elements'. Sufi music is a particular repertoire, composed on the poetry of the Sufiya. It is very subtle, solemn and majestic. So, it is not because there is some ney in it or some specific singing that it's Sufi music. Their music is only dance club music, and that's how it should be seen.

Sometimes some of these musicians feel a bit offended when I say such things, but I don't mean to criticize their music in itself. It isn't my personal taste, but it's the taste of others and that's fine. All I say is that we shouldn't call it Sufi music because it lacks the codes of true Sufi music.

What bothers me a bit, however, is the fact that such practices might become an obstacle for those who are truly interested in Sufism. All these things that dress up as Sufism, while they are not, keep people away from the real thing.

**Is it impossible, then, to find 'the real thing' in Turkey?**

If we want to search for the real literature of the Sufiya, there are, in fact, many works available. You don't have to be a mystic yourself to enjoy the poems of Attar or Rumi. And their works can easily be found, also in translations. The problem is, however, that people don't read Rumi's books. They read the books of others who wrote *about* Rumi. Yet, books *about* the great masters are not the same medicine as the works *of* those great masters themselves.

**I readily agree. Often people don't make the effort to read the classics, even though they contain beautiful treasures. In**

107

Rumi's *Masnavi*,[41] for example, I really love its famous opening verses, the 'song of the reed flute' in which he describes the sound of the ney as an expression of the longing for God. It voices the feeling of separation between the soul and the divine. Is that a feeling you also try to evoke when you play?

The human being has some sort of secret nostalgia within himself. Perhaps the sound of the ney can awake this feeling. But when Rumi speaks of the ney, he does not do so because of its sound. The importance of the ney lies in the fact that it is made from hollow reeds. The metaphor is that those who want to be open to the high inspiration, need to be clean and empty like the insides of the reed flute. You have to become like the ney. You have to let God blow through you.

As such, if there is no ney, you can't properly perform the ceremony because when the ney isn't played, there is separation; when the ney is played, there is unity. Separation is the life of this world. Since we are here, we are in separation, but we have this innate yearning for unity.

The famous Persian poet, Saa'di, described this theme of union and separation most beautifully. He tells the story that he entered the rose garden and saw a nightingale with a rose in his beak lamenting about his separation from the rose. So the poet says to the nightingale: "I don't understand. You are in a rose garden, with a rose in your mouth, but still complain about your separation from the rose." The nightingale replied: "It's a game between us."

---

[41] Rumi's most important work. It will be discussed later in my conversation with Abdulwahid Van Bommel (see p. 153 and the following).

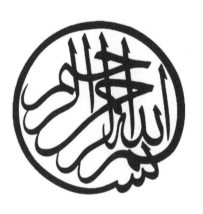

# NORMATIVE
# ISLAM

# ADHAN

The *adhan* is the Islamic call to prayer. It is often a very touching experience to hear it resound all around oneself while it wafts over the rooftops of a Muslim city like a spiritual echo.

I've always experienced it as a very inviting and embracing call to join the Muslims in my vicinity in their prayer. Thus, in my own way, I have often meditated in many mosques. The softness of the rugs on the floor and the roundness of the domes seem to have a soothing and calming effect on my mind, making it easy to slowly descent into an inner depth.

In a sense, this actually symbolizes the essence of my interreligious Halal Monk journey. It wasn't just an effort to start to understand the other. Eventually, it led to a better understanding of myself. By immersing myself in the world of Islam and by getting to know this vast religious reality from the inside, I increasingly wondered how on earth we could arrive at such misrepresentations and misunderstandings.

We cannot quickly answer this question by merely pointing towards 'a lack of knowledge of each other'. It's not as if we lived on separate islands far removed from any possibility of interaction. In fact, the history of the West and Islam are a lot more closely interlocked than people often care to think. The history of Europe, at the very least, has always been intricately connected to the evolutions in the Islamic world, and, as such, we have always 'known' each other.

Not only has there always been a heavy exchange of trade, but there has also been a continuous and elaborate exchange of ideas. The texts of the classical Greek philosophers, to cite one example, came back to the Western world through the writings of Muslim scholars who had heavily expanded on them.

Even seemingly minor details of influence had far-reaching results, such as the fact that the numerals came to Europe through the Islamic civilisation, thus forming the undeniable basis of our current mathematics.

And, of course, there has also always been much political exchange. The Ottoman Empire, for example, was a huge and long lasting neighbour of the European powers. As neighbours, they were certainly often involved in conflicts and wars, but just as much – or perhaps even more – they also had many peaceful and diplomatic relations with various parts of the Western world. In varying measures and forms, therefore, the Ottoman Empire has given and received support from particular kings or states.

———— ✦ ————

We can, of course, also refer to Al-Andalus[42] where Muslims, Jews and Christians lived among each other from the eighth to the fifteenth century. Within their respective communities, they created many great works of art, science, philosophy and theology. This period, when Muslims ruled Al-Andalus, is often called the era of 'convivencia', which is Spanish for 'living together'. It is mostly presented as an idyll of harmony and tolerance between the different religious groups. This shouldn't be exaggerated, however. Often the different communities lived quite separately, not only in

---

[42] Al-Andalus, which is also known as 'Muslim Spain' or 'Islamic Iberia', does not coincide with the contemporary Andalusia but refers to a medieval cultural domain and territory occupying at its peak most of contemporary Spain and Portugal.

their social groups but sometimes even quite literally in separate neighbourhoods. Nevertheless, even though the typical image of Al-Andalus as an exceptionally open and tolerant society asks for quite some nuance, this does not take away from the fact that different religious groups had their accepted place under the Islamic rule. This is in stark contrast with the Christian monoculture that came about as a result of the militaristic Reconquista campaigns. This 'reconquering' of the Iberian Peninsula resulted in the forced conversion, expulsion or execution of almost all Jews and Muslims.

Far too few Europeans are aware of such things. We collectively fail to see our own involvement in the tensions and violence that erupt time and time again. Yet, it is impossible to deny that the Christian world has done much damage to the possibility of peaceful co-existence.

As already mentioned in the introduction, the Crusades are another perfect example thereof. There are many socio-political reasons that called them into existence, and some of these had some legitimacy,[43] but overall, the Crusades were a completely failed attempt to expand Christian lands with an enormous amount of senseless bloodshed as a result.

---------- ❀ ----------

The demonization of Islam, which was prevalent during the time of the Crusades, has never really subsided. Today, we are witnessing just another eruption of the typical image of supposedly aggressive, treacherous and primitive Muslims. Although they have been neighbours for centuries, Europeans still haven't come to recognize them as such. They remain 'the enemy', even to the extent that it blinds us from our own aggression. Within the media,

---

[43] Such as the fact that, at certain times, particular Muslim rulers made it nearly impossible for Christian pilgrims to travel to Jerusalem. Such problems were often removed, however, when the Muslim political leadership of the region changed.

for example, the danger of the slaughter of certain communities is constantly equated with Islam, even though the last genocide that occurred in the heart of Europe murdered thousands of Bosnian Muslims. At the very least, it should make us pause and reflect. Like an inverted adhan, such a historic remembrance invites us to look inward.

We need to ask ourselves some thorough questions and place ourselves within the equation. Where did this aggravating contemporary tension between the West and the East come from? How is it possible that the same degrading views have persisted for centuries? How can it be that we still haven't found our way out of the violence?

Throughout the years, I have come to realise that social and communal conflicts aren't all that different from personal and individual conflicts. In any conflict, both sides have their share in the different actions and reactions, causes and effects. In this respect, innocence and guilt are nothing but faulty terms that do not solve the existing tensions but mostly only aggravate and dichotomize them. And more often than not, the only way out of these tensions is to acknowledge destructive patterns on one's own side.

When we truly wish to get out of our contemporary social conflicts and leave the general mode of confrontation behind, it is high time that the Christian world dares to confront its own patterns and shadows.

To delve deeper into this strange process of cultural self-reflection and to unravel some parts of our collective Christian unconscious, I met with Dr. D. Latifa.

*Photo by Mohammed Anwerzada*

# DR. D. LATIFA

## ON OUR RELIGIOUS SUBCONSCIOUS, THE PROBLEM OF PETRO-ISLAM AND THE DISAPPEARANCE OF MYSTICISM

*Academic, psychologist and feminist. It's never nice to use short labels for uncategorizable people like Dr. D. Latifa,[44] but it sets the tone. For a long time, she was the director of an important research program in a Pakistani university. These days, however, she mainly focuses on her work as a psychologist and her tasks in a centre for the study of gender and culture.*

*If she had to place herself within a certain strand of Western psychology, it would be Jungian psychology, although she can be quite critical about the Jungian approach as well. In fact, being critical is a general aspect of Dr. Latifa's character and, as such, instead of just having a chat for an hour or two, I ended up spending three days with her, discussing various topics related to religion and society. When I eventually headed back home, it was in high spirits and with new insights.*

*What follows is just a small extract of one of our conversations.*

---

❋

---

[44] As Dr. Latifa tries to keep a low profile, certainly considering her stance on certain issues, I changed her name per her request.

**One of the things I noticed while traveling in Pakistan is how closely the Sunni and Shia branches of Islam interlock. I already knew that the current conflicts between the different groups are a very recent development fuelled by the geo-politics of the last fifty years,[45] but I was nevertheless surprised to see how intertwined they were on a daily and spiritual level. Sunni and Shia live side by side, attend each other's festivities and pray at the same shrines. It all makes the current violence seem even more absurd. Do you, as a Pakistani, actually still see a difference between the two?**

In my eyes, one of the great aspects of the Shia tradition is its enormous contribution to passion and love within Islam. In some ways, I actually see this as the main rift between the two branches. As you know, their conflict never was about the Qur'an or the Prophet, but it also wasn't simply about the choice of who would be the next caliph, as it is always presented. According to me, it was also about the way Islam should be *lived*. Of course, every aspect of the Islamic religion can be found in every branch; that is to say, love, fear, jurisprudence, the unity of God and all other core concepts are present in both the Sunni and the Shia theology. However, in a way, the 'psychological approach' of the Shias had a somewhat stronger emphasis on passion while the Sunnis focussed somewhat more on the fear of God, which is, of course, also needed.

---

[45] Throughout the centuries, conflicts between (subgroups of) Sunni and Shia would often surface, but, in spite of what many people think, Sunni and Shia have most often lived peacefully together. As previously mentioned in the explanation on the sharia, the best example thereof is the fact that both Sunni and Shia have always come together for the hajj in Mecca. Because of the geo-politics of the last decades, however, the division has often been rekindled and strengthened to serve other purposes. This can, for example, be seen in the Iran-Iraq war of the 1980s, in the doctrinal radicalisation of the Taliban during the 1990s, and in the insurgences in Syria and Iraq in the 2010s.

**I already discussed the concept of taqwa with Imam Feisal[46] and his spiritual interpretation of it made much sense, but not a lot of your Western psychologist colleagues would easily say that fear is needed – and most certainly not in relation to God.**

There is a cluster of ways to relate ourselves to God. We can do so through fear, love, justice or many other aspects. And within the monotheisms, the aspect of fear also gets a strong emphasis. Look at the Ten Commandments for example; seven of them are about what you will *not* do.

The emphasis in Christianity is on love. In Islam, as a whole, it's on knowledge, if you ask me.

It's not that there's no love in Islam, no knowledge in Judaism or no fear in Christianity, but it's what's emphasized as a profile. It's bland to say that all religions are the same, but when we speak of the differences between different religions, it's not so much about theory or dogmas. It's about the emphasis on a certain aspect of relating to the divine. And whether emphasized or not, fear has its place. It teaches us limits. It makes us recognize that there are lines that we shouldn't cross. One of the biggest examples of the absence of fear is the disastrous situation of the environment, for example. So statements like Roosevelt's, "The only thing you should fear is fear itself", are nonsensical to me. You can't explain to a one year old not to put his fingers in an electrical socket; only fear will teach him not to do it.

I personally think that the West certainly made phenomenal contributions in the realm of the hard sciences, but when it comes to psychology, it's a complete disaster. Western psychology really hasn't gotten far in terms of explaining what human beings are or in grasping the fullness of what they're all about. So, this modern idea that there is no need to fear, for example, is actually an

---

46 See p. 35.

impoverished look on the world.

Also, if you think about it, what has really happened? We are surrounded by fear! Everywhere you go. The present day fear of terrorism is the multiplied version of it. First there was a denial of fear and now we can't escape it. To paraphrase Carl Jung, whatever you deny eventually comes to face you.

**I agree that fear can sometimes give us a proper and even necessary sense of boundaries. But fear, certainly in a religious context, can also be quite stifling.**

Of course context, gender, etc. are very important, but I also think that age is very critical. To encourage a sixteen year old to be fearless is a good thing. To do the same in the case of a fifty year old, I'm not so sure. *(Dr. Latifa laughs.)* Past forty, a lot of issues are actually moral issues, for example. As a psychologist, I think it's important to realize this if you properly want to address certain psychological problems. But modern psychology has no room for that.

Generally speaking, modern psychology is overwhelmingly modelled on the psyches of young males. That is to say, the model of the young male is the archetype. It was Freud's archetype as well, which is all fine for young males, but it simply doesn't work to impose that on women or on men who are in the later stages of life. It doesn't leave enough room for the soul.

**So does religion often come up in your work as a psychologist?**

Again, it depends on the person and his age. There's mostly no point talking religion to a sixteen year old. In fact, it might often be wrong to do so. It's a bit unnatural. But later on, it can certainly come up. Though when people come to me, expecting a psychologist who has studied in Western countries, they mostly don't come to talk about religion.

**Sure, but I also suppose that underneath all their questions, there is some sort of embedded religion and spirituality. At least a lot more than in the West I would think, where religion is, by and large, not at all as embedded in people's minds as it is in the minds of the Pakistanis.**

You're right, but then again, a lot of Christian concepts are strongly anchored in the unconscious of Western people — and not always in a pleasant way. So, when dealing with people who had a highly Western education and who are asking questions about religion, the first task is to get rid of their 'Christianist' unconscious.

I've been fortunate because I spent my schooling first in Anglican schools, in a Catholic convent, an American Presbyterian college – all in Lahore by the way – and, therefore, got to know the whole spectrum. So, I probably know the bible better than most Europeans. And, as such, I think I can fairly judge the depth of the critique of people like Jung. He was right when he said that it's a critical issue today to make people aware of how they think about religion. For our view on religion has fundamentally changed. In the Islamic world as well – because the tragedy is that we're now seeing the worst form of Protestant Christianizing of Islam, though it's dreadfully politically incorrect to say this. *(Dr. Latifa laughs.)*

**Don't bother about political correctness. A good bit of political incorrectness brought about quite a lot of justice throughout history. So, by all means, explain further.**

Well, then, if you ask me, the West is stuck in some sort of 'Cartesian Christianism'. Essentially, it's this Protestant mindset, combined with Cartesianism. By Cartesianism, I mean the rational approach to things, the mental, disembodied and purely analytical way of looking at reality and knowledge.

Combine this puritan 'scientific' approach with a Protestant mindset that holds, at its core, the conviction that only faith in Jesus saves a soul, and what you get is the idea that every question can only have one answer and that everything in existence can be brought back to specific essential parts. In such a worldview, religion becomes something that must, by definition, consist of certain strictly organized convictions and beliefs. But this isn't at all the case in most religions. Also not in Islam, even though the Muslim world, by now, has come to see religion in the same terms.

**This of course relates to your idea that people in the West have lost the capability to think mythologically. You have written about this in some of your essays in which you explain that there are different types of knowledge of which 'logic' is but one. You see 'mytho-logic' as another type. And I must admit that in the West we, indeed, tend to see 'real' knowledge only in logical terms. We ask: "Where do people come from?" and the only answer we expect is: "Out of the fusion of an egg and sperm cell." But many people, me included, derive knowledge about life by relating to stories. As a Christian, for example, I find much more truth and answers about life by 'mirroring' my personal experiences to stories in the Gospels then by reading scientific magazines.**

Indeed. It's the capacity of the symbolic. Science, as it was filtered through modernity, is literal. But when you're drinking water, you're not thinking of it as $H_2O$. It's your experience that matters and that experience can be multiple. So, the meaning of water can be multiple. $H_2O$ has no meaning; it just tells you what the elements in the product are. The tendency is, therefore, to reduce the meaning of everything into its most literal aspect because of the conviction that there is only one answer to things.

Look at the way we nowadays deal with homosexuality, for example. It's clear that the West has brought in a particular view of homosexuality. I guess it partly originates in the way Christ was severed from sexuality in the Christian tradition, as he was considered to be an unmarried celibate. But in certain regions, homosexuality had a place, particularly in those areas that were once a part of Alexander the Great's empire and where the Greek influence was, therefore, evident. In such places, homosexuality could exist side by side with family life. Men simply had certain gatherings – sort of stag nights – once a month or so, in which they could meet other men and have a lot of experiences of male bonding, sometimes also sexually. As long as it didn't threaten the family existence, everyone, including the wife, was okay with it. Again, for the West, you can be only one thing: either homosexual or heterosexual, but here you could have different experiences of reality and sexuality could change during certain life stages.

I keep joking among my friends that within Islamic jurisprudence, people can only be punished for having extramarital sex when there aren't just four witnesses, but four adult, well-respected citizens who are eye witnesses. Now, if you're going to copulate in front of four well-respected citizens, you probably should be stoned. The punishment is more for stupidity than for sin. *(Dr. Latifa laughs.)*

All joking aside, Islam just takes human nature for what it is. So, in Islam, the concept of sin has more to do with hubris and arrogance. When you look at the parameters of the punishment, it seems to me that it says: "Okay, you're going to do this probably, but if you do it, can you please be a bit discrete about it?" So, along with the basic message of 'don't do it' there is also a strong message of 'don't mess with the social order'.

In the non-Western world, then, it has often not been an issue. It even always existed in Arab society. But the minute you ask the question, people will have an opinion and create a 'problem'.

The same happened with family planning and abortion. That

wasn't an issue in the Muslim world before, but it became one after that bizarre coalition in Cairo with the Catholics and the Muslims, because the Catholics went into overdrive and started asking Muslim scholars what their view on abortion was. And, of course, once they were asked, they started to exert their patriarchal views. But that doesn't mean women didn't do it.

Yet another example is the debate about creation versus evolution. I keep telling people that these are false debates that we have internalized. It's not as if Muslims and Hindus didn't have science. These debates stem from mainstream Christian dogmatism, but they were internalized by the Muslim community. In our history, science and religion always went together. But suddenly, certain Muslims feel the need to have an opposite opinion about it — an opinion that coincides with the views of conservative Christians.

**Isn't it remarkable, then, how quickly this 'rational-scientist' and single-minded approach to reality was taken over by other cultural groups in the world? If we look at the modern fundamentalist forms of Islam, for example, we can see that they have taken up the same rhetoric of one single and literal answer to everything. Yet, that sort of contemporary Muslim extremism is an evolution of the last fifty years or so. It is interesting to see, therefore, how quickly people have taken up the Western way of looking at their own religion and how quickly they have forgotten their traditional 'mytho-logical' approach. How come it all happened so fast?**

Well, that's modernity, colonialism and its educational system.

In my own family, religion was always very much a part of our lives. We were encouraged to be modern and get an education, but unlike many middle and higher class Pakistanis and Indians who were enthralled by the Marxist and scientistic worldviews, which were also prevalent in the West, my parents never turned their backs on religion. So, in the nineties, I could see that things had changed quite a bit and that something very wrong was creeping up on us. A rigid mindset that knows only one way of dealing with religion started to take root in our society. Only one particular form of Islam was promoted more and more as the correct form of Islam, even though this wasn't the way we traditionally looked at religion.

Even today, a research showed that if you ask people in India: "What is your religion?" almost three to four million people will name you at least three. So, the fact of the matter is that, as you go down the literacy ladder, there are still huge numbers of people whose self-image, though mostly unconscious, is "I'm a Hindu, I'm a Muslim and I'm a Christian."

**That's indeed something I noticed during my trip through the Punjab and Kashmir region. Religions really get mixed up. And not just as a fact of history, but also in today's reality. Here in Lahore, for example, there's the shrine of Baba Shah Jamal. Every Thursday, people smoke bhang[47] and dance into a trance to the loud beats of the dhol.[48] When I went there, I noticed it actually has a very 'Hindu' feel to it. It's a bit like a loud, colourful Hindu gathering but in honour of a Muslim saint. It made me remember how you once wrote about Lal Ded, the female saint of whom no one actually knew whether she was Muslim or Hindu. In that text, you explained how nobody really cared either and that only now, in the last few decades, many academics suddenly feel the need to prove to which religion she belonged.**

For my generation, such things have been traumatic. My parents were in love with the West and didn't bother any bit about the Christianity they encountered in their lives. Until my father died, in

---

[47] The local cannabis variation.
[48] A dhol is a big barrel-shaped drum. It is a prominent instrument in a lot of Punjabi folk music as well as in contemporary bhangra.

the seventies, my parents still said that if you wanted to see Islam, you had to go to the West. The people there perhaps don't recite the shahada, he said, but they pay their taxes, they're clean, there is social security, and so on. So there was a tremendous admiration for the West. They were devout Muslims, but they never thought twice about me singing Christian hymns at my convent school. They were very happy that good education was given to their children, and they had tremendous respect for the nuns and so on. Nowadays, however, that type of flexibility is being threatened.

**When I speak to people in Pakistan about my work, they all say that they are very religious. Often they add that they're of the Sufi tradition, but above all, they tell me how they respect all religions, how they think all faiths are fine and so on. When I continue the conversation, however, I'll eventually get to a point where they present Islam as the best religion in the world. As such, it quickly became clear to me that they weren't conveying a literal message about the equality of all religions. They above all wanted to distance themselves from the radical Islamists who are, in their eyes, destroying the country. That is to say, they simply don't relate to that single-minded type of Islam that has been imported into Pakistan during the last forty years. How come the Pakistani type of 'blended' Islam with an open-ended view on reality wasn't resilient enough? Why did it not withstand the fundamentalist type?**

On one level, it is still resilient. If the rituals at Shah Jamal can still go on every Thursday, that means it's in fact still very alive. It's our roots. It's the ground beneath our feet.

This is also why I must admit that this whole 'Sufi' business drives me a bit crazy. I first heard the word 'Sufism' when I was forty years old. We saw ourselves simply as Muslims. The word Sufi – or Sufiya, the plural in Arabic – was always traditionally used to describe the saints. But the saints themselves would never say: "I'm a Sufi". They would say: "I'm a Muslim" or "I'm a believer". So, it was a title that expressed respect, but it wasn't a part of our self-definition. So, for me, it makes no sense to say: "Hello, I'm Dr. Latifa, I'm a Sufi."

What is now called Sufism simply was the normative form of Islam. The norm is taken for granted. You don't have to label it. Calling it Sufism only started in the nineties. So it started once the demonizing of Islam began, after the collapse of the Soviet Union. And now, in the same way that children play doctor-doctor, we are now playing Sufi-Sufi. But all this, "oh life is nice, I can listen to music and smoke my dope", that simply isn't what religion is about. It only tries to make it more acceptable to the West.

**I readily agree on this. Sufism is often sold as the 'nice type of Islam', but in the end, it's a term that is used by the West to throw a whole bunch of religious sentiments into one big pot. If it's mystical and Islamic, then it must be Sufism and a bit 'different', so it seems. Yet, as I have come to realise by now, mysticism has always been an essential part of general Islam all over the world and, therefore, knows a huge variety of expressions.**

These are the critical issues that people need to realize because it's all about the lens through which we see religion and it stems from the dominance of Protestant Christianity, which is tied up with the history of religion in the West.

Of course, there has been patriarchy in all religions, but show me one religion that has something comparable to the Inquisition. Or show me one thing that is comparable to the witch hunts. In scale, it is mind blowing when you start reading about it. Wouldn't you say there is something hugely wrong there?

**So what's your answer to that rhetorical question?**

Well, what went wrong was the way they wiped out mysticism in Christianity. And once it was wiped out, the scholars became very surprised when they came across mystical aspects in other religions. Because they marginalised many mystical aspects within Christianity, people today can't understand that those aspects were actually normative to all religions.

The same happens when people think of the way a religion should be structured. In most religions, there simply is no centralized institution. Islam, Buddhism, Hinduism, they're decentred religions. The centre is the individual. So, concepts and words like 'doctrines', 'heresy', 'dogma' all come from Christianity, but then they wanted to apply them to other religions like Islam and say: "Oh, this is the 'dogma' of Islam." Yet decentredness was the natural state of all religions. Yes, you have the Dalai Lama, but he's only there for the Tibetans. He's not there for the Buddhists in Sri Lanka. Protestant Christianity is also decentralized. But eventually, every splinter group of Protestants created its own structures and often held on to very 'single-minded' approaches to reality. Protestants killed a lot more 'witches' than the Catholics did, for example.

And now, vast numbers of Muslims have internalized notions like heresy, doctrine and dogma without wondering: "Is our history the same?"

**The export of the Petro-Islam of the Gulf seems essential in all of this. Even though Islam is still a decentred religion in nature, because of the present day geo-politics that part of the Islamic world has become, to say the least, a very dominant power. I don't think that one could deny that its ideology has widely spread in recent years, and that this ideology contains such a single-minded approach to Islam. But do you think it also holds a true 'structural power' within the broader Ummah? Does it really threaten the decentredness of Islam?**

Yes. They've created the priests since the fifties. Now they will declare Mecca as the Rome of Islam. Perhaps I won't live to see it anymore, but you will.

**I'm reluctant to agree on that one. After all the people I've talked to, I feel that those in power won't be able to hold on to their power like they do now since the dissenting voices are also getting stronger. And not only are their voices getting stronger, they are also becoming a part of the top layers of the ulama.**

They won't be able to extinguish the normative Islam or the dissent of certain intellectuals, but slowly, the space is shrinking and I'm not hopeful at all. This whole region of Southeast Asia will eventually be 'niqabed'. Their work is done. Their mission was to destroy the expressions of normative Islam and they've succeeded.

**Of course, in their own minds they don't see their destruction as something harmful. Quite the contrary, from within their own ideology, they see it as a way of setting things straight.**

Sure. They feel that they're very right, but this is not an ordinary debate of ideas. Where I draw the line is the imposition of a certain lifestyle and way of thinking through brute force. In their case, it's the brute force of money. Their Islam has become a *money*-theism instead of a *mono*-theism.

Let me give you an example of how they gradually 'Arabized' our Islam and started to destroy the local normative expressions of our religion. The standard goodbye for people like me and other Pakistanis of about fifty is "Khudahafiz". Khuda comes from Persian and means 'God' in a very general way. It can imply Allah, but not necessarily. Pakistanis below forty, on the other hand, will say Allahafiz. That's typical Salafi influence and their indoctrination.

So, because of many small things, like how you suddenly say hello and goodbye, I feel like I'm living in an alien place.

**As a Western Christian, I don't easily notice such things, of course. I only see the influence of the Gulf when I pass some mosque that clearly has a different architecture and that is visited by more Salafi-oriented people.**

I have my mad theories, you know. One of them is that the changing mosque architecture shows the change in ideology and spiritual outlook. Not only are those Arab-funded mosques completely un-Pakistani, they're also macho and masculine. The Faisal mosque in Islamabad, which is the biggest mosque in Pakistan, is a good example. It has no curves at all. It has only straight lines with phallic rockets for minarets. You just have to compare it to the old Ottoman mosques in Turkey that have huge beautiful domes. The dome and the minaret were a perfect balance. It's the feminine and the masculine. And often we forget that perhaps the call for prayer is done from the minaret, but it asks you to go into the feminine part of the mosque to actually pray. So, what we're seeing now is the disappearance of the feminine elements and all that we're left with is these jagged lines. You can see the same in the growing use of the Kufic script.
All this Arabizing of our culture is everywhere and it runs very deep.[49]

**I do agree that architecture is very important. I had a teacher once who claimed that trees and complex natural objects like them have some mathematical 'formulas' behind them, but that those 'formulas' are equations that create infinitely irregular forms. He added that today's city architecture takes**

---

[49] Dr. D. Latifa talks about Pakistan here, but the same phenomenon of 'Arabisation' can be witnessed in many parts of the Muslim world from Somalia to Indonesia and certainly within migrant communities as well.

**away our capacity to deal with such complex and irregular forms and formulas. According to him, it impoverishes our minds when our surroundings only consist of straight lines because all our streets are straight and our buildings are nothing but cubes put on top of each other.**

I call such buildings anorexic. They reflect the state of the anima. The feminine is starving in the modern world. It's dying — as is nature.

We can see the same in interior design. It's all minimalist, clean, cold, straight lines. It's often sold as Zen, but it's not the same. Zen is a state of mind, but this modern style is often simply soulless.

**True. Real Zen is about inner peace. In its art, one can, therefore, see many curves, circles and waves . . . But to come back to the 'Arabisation' of Pakistan, it might be very visible in the architecture and art, but does that necessarily mean it also has a strong impact on daily life? Does it truly also take away certain 'feminine' aspects of society?**

Of course. That's exactly what's under attack. Mysticism is a female dimension of every religion, while the scriptural is the more masculine. And this is yet another example of how the Christian Cartesian mindset has taken over the Islamic world as well. The scriptural, the literal and the puritan become the norm. Everything else is considered 'pagan' – and again, paganism is, of course, a Christian term for what used to be indigenous, natural religions lived and practiced without a structure being imposed on them.

So, my problem is how to get out of that vocabulary and reclaim a different view on religion because there are a lot of Muslims these days who say that several traditional elements aren't a part of 'pure' Islam. Certainly, in the diaspora you can often hear it, because the migrants have been cut off from their culture. But the very reason why Islam took wings and spread so rapidly is because it could adapt itself to different cultures.

If we look at history, we can see that Islam had reached its borders within a hundred years. So, it only took a century for Islam to spread out to Spain, Asia and China. I often joke that that this means that God wanted to say: "Get out of the Middle East as fast as you can!" *(Dr. Latifa laughs.)*

But seriously, even today, only fifteen per cent of Muslims live in the Middle East. Eighty-five per cent are elsewhere. And if we look at the art and architecture, we can see how it has flourished because of the way it always bonded with culture.

If Islam didn't have that openness and simplicity, we wouldn't have had the Alhambra or Sultan Ahmet Mosque. They're so different, but both are Islamic. And this multiplicity of expressions of the same faith is, in fact, the strength and beauty of Islam.

# SALAM

Those who start studying the Islamic tradition quickly come to know that the word '*salam*', which means peace, comes from the same linguistic root as the word 'Islam'. On the other hand, they will also learn that the literal translation of the word 'Islam' means 'surrender' or 'submission'. Muslim scholars who want to show Islam at its most beautiful will emphasize the underlying root of peace. Critics of Islam, however, will put a focus on the word 'submission' as this word arouses a sense of distrust in the ears of many secular Westerners. To them, the word 'submission' seems to indicate that this religion is, indeed, some sort of opium of the people.

Being a theologian myself – albeit Christian – I've always found an incorrect interpretation of the word 'submission' a sad mistake. The true meaning implies 'surrender to the divine undercurrent of existence', which is a very beautiful and even fundamental spiritual concept in many traditions. Its connection to the concept of peace isn't all that difficult to understand either. In fact, a similar relationship is acknowledged in the English language in the expression, 'to be at peace with something'. The idiom, 'to be at peace with something', means to accept a certain reality we were confronted with. Or, more precisely, to 'surrender' to a certain situation in such a way that it makes the tensions, which were in the way of our acceptance, disappear.

Throughout history, there have been lots of discussions about the words 'Islam' and 'salam', and many scholars offered different nuances. Yet, it does not seem necessary to read all those treatises in order to understand this one particular aspect. Even more so, for Arabic speakers specifically, the connection between peace and surrender is clear from the start since the similar sound of the words and the linguistic link of the root consonants 's', 'l' and 'm' immediately brings about the association.

Therefore, the true 'submission to God', which lies at the core of Islam, doesn't come about because the Prophet said to do so, because the Qur'an obliges it, or simply because tradition prescribes it. No; one gives oneself to God because one is 'at peace with it' – that is to say, at peace with the idea that only a focus on the divine can eventually offer spiritual freedom, and that a focus on our ego will only keep us imprisoned within ourselves.

As such, the word 'Islam' does not mean a sort of 'submission' that puts all critical thinking aside, like many Islamophobes often claim it does. It's also quite something else than the 'surrender' that mainly occupies itself with strictly following some rules and regulations, like certain Muslim preachers seem to interpret it. For above all, it's a spiritual submission to the divine flow of life which brings peace to the soul.

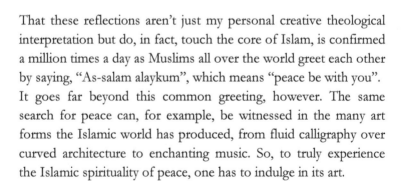

That these reflections aren't just my personal creative theological interpretation but do, in fact, touch the core of Islam, is confirmed a million times a day as Muslims all over the world greet each other by saying, "As-salam alaykum", which means "peace be with you".

It goes far beyond this common greeting, however. The same search for peace can, for example, be witnessed in the many art forms the Islamic world has produced, from fluid calligraphy over curved architecture to enchanting music. So, to truly experience the Islamic spirituality of peace, one has to indulge in its art.

One specific Islamic art form that has done particularly well among people who don't have roots within Islam is the devotional music of Pakistan called *qawwali*. It's a form of spiritual praise in which mystical poetry is sung against the backdrop of a harmonium, tabla and clapping. The iconic Nusrat Fateh Ali Khan brought this qawwali to many festivals and art centres and, thus, acquainted many people with this very vivid expression of what Dr. D. Latifa called 'normative Islam'. He died in 1997, but this particular art form certainly didn't. People, such as his captivating nephew Muazzam and the ever impressive Abida Parveen, for instance, remain figureheads of this intoxicating musical devotion, spreading its message of peace all over the globe.

# ABIDA PARVEEN
# & MUAZZAM FATEH ALI KHAN
## ON THE RHYTHMIC HEART
## OF RELIGION

*Abida Parveen is one of the foremost exponents of devotional music worldwide. Some years ago, a music journalist from the BBC wrote that she could sing a shopping list and still have an audience weeping. And sure enough, even when people don't understand a word of the old verses about longing for unity with the divine, Abida is capable of touching the depths of their souls.*

*When I met her, it quickly became clear that it wasn't only her voice that mesmerizes people. Her whole personality is capable of doing so, for behind her genuine humbleness, I could immediately sense a thoroughly embedded spirituality.*

*I encountered a very similar spirituality when I met Muazzam Fateh Ali Khan. Perhaps more than any other contemporary qawwali singer, Muazzam keeps the legacy and spirit of his uncle Nusrat alive, not only through his recordings and performances of classical qawwali, but also through contemporary fusions with electronic music.*

*I met both artists independently. Abida received me in her home in Islamabad, Muazzam in his house in Feisalabad. Yet, because what they had to say coincided in many ways, I bring these two conversations together as if they were both present in the same room.*

**Let us, perhaps, start from the very core of the matter. What do you feel is the essence of qawwali or, more generally, of Pakistani devotional music?**

*Abida:* The word 'qawwali', in fact, is derived from the Arabic word 'qaul', which means 'saying' or 'quotation'. That's because our devotional music always tries to transfer a deeper meaning. It isn't just some frivolous music. That's why we also don't say we 'sing' qawwali or *sufiana kalam*.[50] We say we 'do' it. We 'recite' it.

*Muazzam:* Of course, every style of music has its own value, but what makes qawwali into qawwali is the fact that it's the music which is linked to the Sufi saints. That's why Abida says we 'recite' their verses more then we sing them.

**On the other hand, the content of the lyrics isn't the only aspect of importance. The musical aspect also has its very own character, does it not?**

*Abida:* Indeed. Amir Khusrow, who is regarded as the inventor of qawwali, knew the classical music of his days very well, so he used it to decorate his words and make them more beautiful through the use of music. His main goal was to transfer certain messages or sayings. Besides expressing these messages in words, he gave a musical expression to their emotional content. For example, when the poetry spoke of spring, he knew how to translate the emotion of spring into music. Because of this, he could touch the hearts of the people more easily, yet everything he did was always connected to a deeper spirituality.

---

[50] Qawwali and sufiana kalam are related forms of devotional music. The differences can be found in their particular set-up. Sufiana kalam will be performed by one particular singer, backed up by just one or a couple of musicians. Qawwali, on the other hand, is always performed in a group, mostly of nine to twelve people, consisting of a lead singer with several backing vocals, supported by a percussionist and a harmonium player.

## What deeper spirituality is that?

*Abida:* One of the core elements of this spirituality is what is called the most famous qaul of qawwali: "Man kunto maula fahaza Ali un maula." It means: "When you accept me as your master, then Ali is your master, too." This is a hadith of the Prophet, peace be upon him. He made this announcement after he did the hajj. It is said that, on a certain day, he stopped his companions at Khadir and asked them to make a podium so he could stand on it and address the people. When he stepped on the podium, he made this announcement, which wasn't just a technical announcement. It was a miracle of God. It was a message that God provided *through* the words of the Prophet. So, within this verse lies the secret of our universe.

Amir Khusrow understood this so well that this qaul became the backbone of his qawwali. There are two reasons for this. The first is that the brotherhood and love that the Prophet showed for Ali at that very moment became a source of inspiration. The soulful connection that the Prophet portrayed there and then is an example of how we should all relate to each other. The second reason is that it explains how we have to look at Ali to see what it means to excel as a human. Ali's deep spirituality is an example of how we should all try to be spiritual. That's why that one sentence became the foundation of our devotional music and why the basic purpose of our music is to preach love, brotherhood, and humanity.

**You now present Pakistani devotional music as something that is used to spread 'general human values'. Yet, does it not also specifically try to convey the message of Islam to a broader public?**

*Abida:* One of the aims of God, the prophets and the saints is to 'upgrade' humanity and human beings. You can improve yourself and your soul by listening to the words of the saints. But their words speak about spirituality and mysticism. What they say is above religion, for in spirituality, religion shouldn't matter. In that sense, true Islam is for everyone. It's not a religion for a specific group of people. Islam is a gift from God to the whole of humanity. Islam is not prejudiced. Wherever people are doing good deeds, there is Islam. Wherever you find good things, it's Islam. Whenever you think something is good, it's Islam.

So Islam is about love, brotherhood and being unified. And it was the function of the saints to spread and announce the message and the mystic spirituality of Islam. Whatever they did, they did it from their hearts. That is why they constantly spoke about the importance of the connection between humans and God.

**So Muazzam, is there some verse of the saints that speaks of such unity which is particularly dear to your heart?**

*Muazzam:* One phrase that is very dear to me, for example, is: "Main to piya se naina mila rahi", which you could translate as: "I'm going to make eye contact with my lover." Though whatever I sing, the moment I sing it, it fills my spirit.

In qawwali, we often sing a mix of languages. It can go from Urdu to Punjabi to Persian. The audience often doesn't understand the language, but they can feel the spirit if it's properly performed. And you can only perform it properly if you're completely 'involved' in the words. The singer has to be fully devoted to the saint and his messages at the moment he's singing in order to truly convey the words.

I'll give you an example of how deeply the words can penetrate one's soul. One day, Fateh Ali Khan, the father of Nusrat, was singing with Mubarak, my grandfather. All of a sudden, he closed his eyes, his face became red and he started shaking like a bird. He then tore off his clothes and left the qawwali group while the rest played on. He ran for one kilometre at 2 am at night and jumped into a canal. People took him out and noticed his body was still burning hot. They brought him home and, after one and a half hours, he awoke. They asked him what had happened, but he said he didn't know because he was in a different state of mind. Our father was also present that night. He told us the story.

**In the West as well, more and more people have heard of the message of unity and the trance-inducing effect of qawwali music. But, at the same time, when Pakistan is mentioned in the news, it is often in relation to terrorism and violent extremism. The beautiful art forms of Pakistan, like qawwali, receive very little attention. I have met many Pakistanis who feel very frustrated about this. I guess you, as a traditional qawwali singer, know this frustration as well.**

*Muazzam:* Absolutely. If Muslims were terrorists, that would be a huge problem. If all those hundreds of thousands of people who go to shrines of the great saints, such as Data Ganj Bakhsh or Lal Shahbaz Qalandar, were all terrorists, that would be terrifying.

But the Sufiya are the people who 'pleased God' and God was with them. God asked people to go to the saints before you go to Him. So, if all those people go to the shrines of saints and pray to the Prophet and his family who were spreading God's message, they can't all be terrorists.

The Prophet also said that you cannot convert someone to be a Muslim by force. If you think Islam is wrong, you don't have to accept it. If you think it's right, you have to. That's the reality of Islam. The Prophet asked for love and peace and the Ummah should follow what he asked for. So, Islam brings a message of peace. Terrorism has nothing to do with real Islam. It's all planned by people who are interested in things other than real religion.

**Is qawwali itself under threat because of the fundamentalists and terrorists you referred to? Since many of them hold the**

opinion that music is haram, their violence might be directed at artists like you as well.

*Muazzam:* We don't have a problem yet, but when they start criticizing what we do, we'll have a very good answer ready for them. Our answer comes from the hadith. When the Prophet, peace be upon him, migrated to Medina, the girls of Medina made tambourines, came out of their houses and sang songs. Some people asked the Prophet whether it wasn't *shirk*.[51] The Prophet replied: "Keep quiet. They're doing this because they're so happy and because they want to make the Prophet happy. Their happiness is more important for me than your objection."
If music was haram, the Prophet would have stopped the girls at that time. The Prophet and the saints followed God, so if it were wrong, they would have gotten rid of it. But, by now, qawwali has been in practice for the last thousand years. It was important before and will have a bright future long after we die.

**And did you, Abida, ever experience any problems in Pakistan – which is quite patriarchal on many levels – because you are a female singer?**

*Abida:* No, not at all.

**So what about the reverse? Did the fact that you are a female singer give you a special bond with female Sufiya, such as Rabia, for example?**

*Abida:* All saints reached a great level. It's not up to me to say who is higher and who is lower. I have no status to distinguish between superior and inferior. And within the higher spirituality of the Sufi saints, male or female also loses its meaning. They own the

---

[51] Shirk means creating an idol and worshipping something or someone other than God.

spiritual world and the spiritual world is there because of them. They're all imams who lead the whole of humanity. And I follow them.

**Yet, as you explained, Ali retains a specific place in your tradition. So, do you two have a special connection to him, not only on a spiritual level but also as singers?**

*Abida:* Of course; Ali is my guide and without the presence of my guide, I cannot sing or recite! I have to 'see' him before I can start. Like God is present, Ali is present.

*Muazzam:* You know, there are certain personalities like the *Panjtan Pak*[52] who transcend us all but it depends how we go to them. If we love, admire and follow them, we will feel that they're with us. If not, we won't feel them. So, in the case of Ali, yes, he received the title 'lion of God' and whenever we need help and call him, he will help us.

---

[52] Panjtan Pak is an Urdu word that combines Prophet Mohammad, Ali (the Prophet's nephew and son-in-law), Fatimah (the wife of Ali and daughter of the Prophet), Hassan (the first son of Ali and Fatimah) and Hussain (the second son of Ali and Fatimah).

# FANA

*Fana* is a less known aspect of Islamic theology. It means 'passing away', 'annihilation' or 'evaporation' and, as such, is a term the mystics used to describe the spiritual point where the ego is finally removed and unity with the divine is achieved.

It is concepts like these that make it amply clear how Islam has always been a bridge between the East and the West as it connects two different approaches towards the divine. In a sense, the Far East has a far more impersonal view of the divine. They speak of an ultimately indescribable eternal whole which envelops and pervades everything. The divine is seen as the ultimate core of existence that 'flows' through the whole of existence. They, therefore, speak of an 'It' rather than a 'Him' to refer to the divine. The Abrahamic religions, on the other hand, hold a more personal view of God. He 'created' rather than 'emanated' and, although He's certainly also present within the world, He is always transcendent and, therefore, ultimately 'different'.

Just like any generalisation, this distinction is overly crude and many counterexamples can be found. We can easily discover impersonal approaches within the Abrahamic religions, and we can just as easily come across personal approaches in Hindu traditions. It is not a strict division, therefore, but rather an 'emphasis' or a certain 'dominant approach' in the different cultural spheres. In other words, we shouldn't see them as two excluding views but more as two poles on a continuum of options. And between those two poles, one can find many variations that often fuse them in brilliant ways.

The Sufiya are good examples of such a fusion. Their mysticism and their poetry often speak of a personal love which, like an outstretched hand, reaches for unity with the Beloved. Nonetheless, eventually a fana can be reached, thereby completely dissolving the ego and embalming the soul by the divine whole. The teachings of many Sufiya are, therefore, full of elements that can be found in Judaism and Christianity, even though they're also replete with concepts that relate closely to Buddhism and Hinduism.

---

Such a hybrid spirituality can also be found in the teachings of Mevlana Rumi, who has already been mentioned in several conversations. But Rumi certainly isn't the only one of his kind. The history of Islam contains an enormously long list of such sages and saints. Junaid, Rabia, Ghazali, Hafez, Bulleh Shah, Al Hallaj, Amir Khusrow, Yunus Emre . . . We could go on for quite some time. In this book, however, I'll stick to Rumi. I'll do so for a couple of reasons.

First of all, as was already mentioned, Rumi's poetry is hugely popular in the West.

Second, although his familiarity is a benefit, the contemporary image of Rumi is in need of some correction. He's sometimes presented, for example, as the 'unexpected' Muslim mystic. But Rumi is not a modern or bizarre 'discovery' at all. From Turkey to India, many Muslims have always known his words and verses by heart, not in the least because a lot of those verses became daily idioms.

That is also why he was already mentioned in many of the previous conversations and why he will come up yet again in many of the following conversations. His impact on literature and thought in the Islamic world has simply been quite pervasive. So, from Karachi to New York, many people are acquainted with Rumi and the whirling dervishes of his order.

Some have also come to know a bit more about the bond of transcendent love between Rumi and Shams, his teacher and close companion. When Shams disappeared, so the traditional story goes, Rumi went on a spiritual quest which eventually resulted in fana.

This gives us yet another good reason to delve deeper into the spirituality of Rumi's 'normative Islam', for this poet and preacher was an undeniable master of the spirituality of ego-transcendence. And that seems to be exactly what we need ever more today — not only on an individual and spiritual level but also on a communal and social level. Finding ways to transcend our egos is a necessity for society as a whole.

In this respect, it is good to realise that Rumi himself also lived in a time of much conflict. On top of this, he lived on the border of the Islamic world. In fact, that's where he got his name from, for the area at the border with the Byzantine Empire was called 'Rum'.[53] This means that Rumi was fully aware of what cultural tension and conflict could entail. His teachings can, therefore, offer quite a lot of insights about today's global situation.

———— ❖ ————

People often only read Rumi's mystical love poems. His greatest work is the *Masnavi*, however, which is an elaborate 'educational poem'. It's one of the most important mystical works in the history of Islam in particular and religion in general. I, therefore, went to

[53] 'Rum' is not an Arabic word but is connected to the word 'Roman'. The word 'mevlana', on the other hand, comes from Persian and means 'master' or 'teacher'. So the way we know Rumi nowadays is actually as 'the spiritual master of the Byzantine region'. His original name was Jelal Al Din Muhammad Balkhi.

see Abdulwahid Van Bommel, one of its contemporary translators, to unravel some of its secrets and to discover what it can still teach all of us.

*Photo by Mark Kohn*

# ABDULWAHID VAN BOMMEL
# ON RUMI AND THE SECRET
# OF HIS MASNAVI

*Hanging out with hippies and beatniks, devouring literature, playing bass in a jazz band, memorising quotes of the Tao-Te-Ching and becoming a Muslim in the Moluk community in July '67. I've put these elements in random order as a quick sketch of Abdulwahid Van Bommel's younger years. The end result of it all was that he found his spiritual home in the mystical traditions of Islam. Because of that, he stayed in Turkey for four years as a student and member of the Naqshbandi brotherhood.*[54]

*When he returned to the Netherlands, he gradually became a key figure in the Dutch Muslim community. Eventually, a few years ago, a Turkish friend asked him whether he didn't want to translate Rumi's Masnavi. At first, he hesitated, but three years later, the very first Dutch translation of the more than twenty-five thousand verses was a fact.*

---

[54] The Naqshbandi brotherhood is a Sufi tariqa that originated in the twelfth century out of the teachings of Yusuf Hamdani and Abdul Khaliq Gajadwani. The latter is regarded as the shaykh who introduced the silent *dhikr*, one of the practices which is typical of the Naqshbandi. Dhikr is an Islamic devotional act and method of prayer that shows a lot of similarities with the repetition of mantras. It typically involves the recitation of the Names of God and/or supplications taken from hadith or Qur'anic verses. It can be translated as 'remembrance'. The practice is, therefore, seen as a way of constantly remembering God. Whereas dhikr will be performed out loud in many tariqas, the Naqshbandi remain quiet when repeating their specific devotional phrases.

**Rumi wrote in the thirteenth century, yet the *Masnavi* still seems to have much relevance in these times of quick cultural changes.**

Indeed. Rumi's time and age was quite like ours. You had the Seljuks, the Mongols, the Byzantines, the Persians and the Arabs, who all fought each other. And in between all political upheaval was a lot of cultural exchange.

You have to imagine that Baghdad was conquered by the Mongols in Rumi's time, which must have had an enormous influence on the Muslims of his area. Yet, you won't read a word about it in his writings. He was very much aware of it since he belonged to that layer of society who were the first to hear about such things, but strangely enough, in his own works, he doesn't mention it.

I think it was his way of trying to 'keep the balance', to uphold that equilibrium on a global scale in which one thing always invokes another. So, he didn't just build a worldview, but he came up with an internalized worldview that stays away from the corrupt world of war and violence.

He created a world in which we, as humans, can all feel connected to the cosmos. All the elements we find in the cosmos are present within the human being. So, we all are a small cosmos on our own. Nowadays, scientists say the same thing, but Rumi realized it out of some mystical intuition.

Rumi brings deep mysticism to the people. That's why he uses all the existing stylistic devices in the many anecdotes and stories of the *Masnavi*, but they are also followed by reflections that explain in long abstract reasonings how we are all one with God and how everything is unified. In that way, he offered a counterbalance to all the dinginess around us of always wanting to have-have-have. He opposed it with a mode of being that helps one to totally detach from it all.

**Sometimes it, indeed, seems completely useless to constantly**

restart the 'societal fight'. The same discussions are often repeated and I sometimes feel it's better to simply point towards the spiritual dimension of existence and then leave it to the individual to decide what he or she wishes to take from it.

That's true, but on the other hand, certainly in these times, we shouldn't forget to keep an eye open on everything around us. We must keep our minds open to different philosophies, worldviews and elements of society. That brings a certain solidity in our thinking. The gnostic of the world is the gnostic of God.

That's true. It simply remains a difficult discussion. Do you leave the chaos aside or do you take up the effort to try to bring some peace into it? To flee from the world has no use, but neither is it good to lose oneself in that world.

Rumi actually found some balance in that dilemma. He did confront the chaotic world of desire, greed and war with a spiritual process of 'internalization', but he also tried to bring that process as close as he could to the people. For him, 'being spiritual' isn't reserved for intellectuals or especially gifted people. That's why he made it clear how your spirituality should bring you to the centre of reality and that you shouldn't turn your back to the world.

Ultimately, Rumi is a humanist. He wants to tell people that 'meaning something to someone' is the highest good.

Nonetheless, although we can find such a 'humanism' in his writings, doesn't Rumi above all focus on a strong 'divinism'? I invent the word somewhat, but I use it to refer to his constant striving for total unification with the divine.

I have to admit that I initially was quite sceptical about Rumi and his view on this matter. I had some resistance towards such a goal, for in Sufism there's a difference between *wahdat al-wujud* and *wahdat ash-shuhud*.

According to the wahdat ash-shuhud – the idea of unity of perception, of which Ahmad Sirhindi is an important proponent – one can eventually only be a 'witness' of the divine. There remains a distinction between yourself and God and your connection to God is somewhat more 'from the outside'. But in the wahdat al-wujud, they propose that total unification with the divine is possible. The Spanish Sufi, Ibn Arabi, is seen as an important promoter of this teaching. I am a Naqshbandi myself, however, and that school of thought belongs to the wahdat ash-shuhud, so my view on the matter differed from Rumi's.

Yet, when you start reading Rumi's texts, he takes you along and something happens to you. One way or the other, my resistance fell away and I experienced a deep unity.

## So, did you eventually choose 'the way of total unification'?

In the end, it's not really a matter of choosing one or the other. There might be different interpretations about the *nature* of the divine unity, but there is no doubt about the *fact* of divine unity. And it increasingly becomes clear to me how little difference there is between those two paths. All in all, it's a very thin line that dissolves the moment you truly experience it. But you almost can't express that experience with words.

What is so wondrous about Rumi, therefore, is the fact that he took up the fight to try to express the inexpressible. He tries to describe the essence of what moves us in our depth, what emotionally and spiritually makes us human.

Something that, for example, really stuck in my mind was the thought that "the heart of the one who hasn't crossed his own boundaries, still lies at the feet of the other." Such an insight is not just a nice slogan. It expresses a different reality. It points towards the difference between love of the senses and spiritual love. Love of the senses is love for what you see, hear, feel, experience, etc. Spiritual love means to partake in the universal love. Spiritual love is a reality that is joined by the whole of creation. It is not possessive. While all mental and organic love has something possessive and claims or demands something, spiritual love has none of that. Spiritual love goes beyond the individual. It is experienced 'personally' but it's not private or personal.

Rumi, therefore, also doesn't want to be occupied with spirituality in a bit of a bourgeois way. It's a very serious matter for him and he wants to bring everyone to pure unity of love.

**On the other hand, it isn't always strict seriousness. The *Masnavi* is also known for its funny anecdotes.**

Even more so, sometimes those tales are quite erotic as well. That's why the *Masnavi* is forbidden in certain circles. There is quite a daring scene, for example, in which a maid has found a way of having fun with the donkey in the stable. On a certain day, the lady of the house discovers her secret. Yet, the very sight of it brings a whole lot of phantasies to her own mind as well. So, she sends the maid on an errand and goes to the stable in excitement. What she hadn't seen, however, is how the maid always slid a pumpkin around the penis of the donkey to make sure that its length was shortened. So, when the lady of the house approaches the donkey, she gets killed relentlessly the moment the donkey takes her fully. *(Abdulwahid laughs.)*

**That's a fantastic story, if for nothing else, because it's a part of such a world-famous mystical text. But what does it mean according to you? Is its message simply that we should learn to control our desire?**

That's a part of it, but a different layer of its meaning, I think, is that you shouldn't just follow any role model. In the Muslim world, that's often made very attractive, but Rumi makes it clear that you shouldn't thoughtlessly mimic someone. You always have to comprehend how and why you have to do something. So you shouldn't simply imitate a prophet or a saint.

Like this, Rumi's stories have little fishing hooks. Like needles, they stick to your mind.

**Is there another specific story that stuck to your mind like that?**

One story I really love tells about a scholar who passes a lake on a little ferryboat. The scholar hears the grammatical mistakes the ferryman is making and at a certain moment asks: "Did you actually finish your schooling?" The ferryman answers: "No, I haven't gotten around to it because I had to work." "Ah", the scholar says, "then half of your life has been a waste." Like that, they peddle along, but in the middle of the lake, it turns out that the boat doesn't have a very good bottom. Slowly, it starts sinking. At that moment, the ferryman asks the scholar: "Say, did you actually learn to swim?" The scholar answers: "No, I haven't because I had to study." "Ah," the ferryman says, "then your whole life was a waste."

**This is, indeed, a great example of how Rumi often questioned all forms of authority – whether on a political or a scholarly level. I always love the way he puts great emphasis on the idea that status doesn't matter in the direct connection between the individual and God. Sadly enough, however, the brotherhoods that stemmed from Rumi and other Sufiya sometimes got taken up in the existing structures of society and, gradually, certain hierarchies crept in.**

That's true. And when certain groups couldn't claim a societal status, they sometimes sought to confirm their hierarchy in the 'spiritual world' in the sense that they tried to show how they are the only ones who will be saved. So, their language of the hereafter became stronger, because if you don't have a hierarchy on earth you can always focus on a theoretical hierarchy in heaven.

That's, of course, not something specific for the followers of the Sufis. One can see, for example, that it's also very attractive for young people in the West. In the Netherlands Muslim migrants often don't get many chances in the job market. It's quite difficult for them to earn a good status in society. And then you get phenomena, such as the fundies of Sharia4UK, Sharia4Holland and Sharia4Belgium. When you listen to their language and creeds, you can immediately hear how narrow-minded they are and how little they have comprehended what Islam really teaches, but they do attract youngsters who are excited by gatherings at 'secret places'. In such groups, they receive a certain meaning within the hierarchy they create for themselves.

All of that sharply contrasts with Rumi's *Masnavi*. His own Mevlevi order was strongly structured after he died, but that was because of his son, Sultan Valad. In his own texts, you won't find any hierarchy because Rumi actually takes the same stance Nelson Mandela once expressed when he said: "A saint is a sinner that keeps on trying." Every time we wind up in the gutter, we can get up again. That's Rumi's vision. So, he didn't propose any plan with different levels. He realized that people make many mistakes but can also always stand up and once more embark on the search for unification.

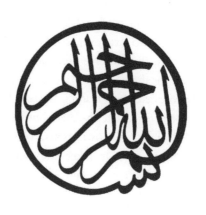

# CONSTRUCTIVE
# DISSENT

# HIJAB

Patriarchy is a problem. It's a problem all over the world and within most, if not all, communities and cultures. But somehow, the discussions on patriarchy are often narrowed down to the Muslim world. The worldwide discussions on headscarves and veils are a perfect example thereof. From America to Turkey to Afghanistan, one of the most common debates on culture and religion is the debate on the attire of Muslim women. Whether it's in the context of the integration of Muslim minorities or whether it's in the framework of the War on Terror, hijabs,[55] niqabs[56] and burqas[57] have become strong symbols of our contemporary cultural tensions.

I will not go into the theological details of the veiling of women. It suffices to say that many scholars are divided in their particular views on the matter, the result being that throughout history a huge variety of veils and scarves have been worn (or not worn) for different reasons. Some wear (or don't wear) their particular piece of head covering simply as a custom of their culture, others because they feel it's a religious duty, still others because of a political statement and still others because of the prevalent fashion. Of course, in particular times and places, there has also been social

---

[55] A hijab is the common headscarf, which covers the hair.
[56] A niqab is a veil that covers everything except the eyes.
[57] A burqa is a long, loose garment covering the whole body from head to feet.

or political pressure on women to cover themselves. However, for non-Muslim communities to suddenly see this piece of attire as the very pinnacle of female suppression exerted by an inherently patriarchal structure called Islam, is somewhat remarkable. Certainly when such discussions take place in regions with a Christian background because the cultural memory of Christian countries is replete with headscarves since Mother Mary, who is abundantly present in their art and folklore is quite consistently depicted wearing a headscarf. Nevertheless, we never hear anyone say that Mother Mary was oppressed by a patriarchal Judaism.

———————— ❁ ————————

The secular minds that obsessively plead for a ban on headscarves in public settings actually don't differ that much from the religious extremists who would like to cover every woman they come across. Both types of men try to determine what women should or shouldn't do.

According to staunch religious fundamentalists, headscarves or veils are a religious edict that cannot be discussed or questioned. They, therefore, continuously rant about how every pious woman should be properly dressed. But what about those women who are modestly dressed without a headscarf? And what about those women who have always upheld the five pillars of Islam but simply couldn't care less about their specific clothing?

In the eyes of modernist Islamophobes, on the other hand, veils and headscarves can be nothing else but a form of female oppression that prevents women from showing their feminine sensuality. They, therefore, continuously rant about how women should be freed and empowered. But what about those women who freely choose to wear a headscarf? And what about those women who combine individual expression and religious tradition by wearing their own particular style of headscarf?

On the streets of Brussels as well as Istanbul, one can see very fashionable headscarves everywhere. Many veiled women wear their bright scarves in a way that certainly would not upset any Versace. Like many non-Muslim women, they simply try to look as good as they can, and their veil is certainly not ruining those efforts.

But then other critics pop up and say that wearing the headscarf in such a manner is hypocritical. An item traditionally used to make a woman less of a sexual object has now become an extension of their attractiveness.

And, thus, they get stuck between hammer and anvil. In whatever way they wear (or don't wear) the headscarf, the whole discussion leads to a dead end. In fact, it's not a discussion. It's a trap set by men to trap other men. And the bait is women.

One side says: "The way you force your women to look is oppressive and intolerable." The other side says: "Wearing a veil is a religious duty, and it's intolerable to take away their freedom of religion." Yet, the only thing that is truly intolerable is the way women are volleyed around like a ping pong ball.

In the end, neither type of man is capable of letting women choose for themselves and letting them radiate strength within that choice. Both sides use a symbol with variable meanings for personal or political purposes.

The headscarf, which can be worn for many different reasons, is not a problem in itself. But acting as if the headscarf has a singular meaning is.

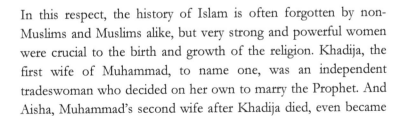

In this respect, the history of Islam is often forgotten by non-Muslims and Muslims alike, but very strong and powerful women were crucial to the birth and growth of the religion. Khadija, the first wife of Muhammad, to name one, was an independent tradeswoman who decided on her own to marry the Prophet. And Aisha, Muhammad's second wife after Khadija died, even became the leader of the first Muslim army.

All through history, impressive women can be found and today as well, there certainly isn't any lack of them. One simply needs to be willing to look for them and listen to what they have to say.

In spite of the image projected by much of the general media and in spite of the loudness of overly-conservative preachers, Muslim women certainly aren't always and everywhere the poor helpless victims of angry bearded men. They often vigorously stand up. A concept like 'Islamic feminism' is, therefore, difficult to grasp for many people and, as such, often ignored. Because of its prejudices, the modernist mindset isn't capable of framing feminist Muslims as 'real Muslims', while the reactionary traditionalist mindset isn't capable of seeing them as 'truly faithful'. But whether they're capable of understanding it or not, feminists are an undeniable part of the contemporary Ummah, and Muslim feminism is an increasingly strong aspect of present day Islam.

Amina Wadud is a leading figure within that movement, and she certainly doesn't have to be 'freed' from her religion. She doesn't need modernist or secular men to get rid of what supposedly suppresses her. Quite the contrary; it's exactly her faith that gives her the power to fight both Islamic and modernist patriarchies.

A lot of controversy arose when Amina started to lead the prayer in her home town mosque – which, of course, meant that men were sitting behind her and were following her ritualistic instructions. Many conservative authorities in different parts of the world denounced her act and cried foul. But however loud some of them might have shouted that she's a heretic, Amina Wadud remains a very serious and well-respected scholar in many circles. She has helped and encouraged a large number of women's groups, and her books are read by many Muslim women all around the world who are very active on different social and political levels.

# Amina Wadud
# on Islamic feminism
# and reformed theology

*Few people combine solid academics with strong activism and gentle spirituality as smoothly as Amina Wadud. She's the daughter of a Methodist minister, but this feisty American woman converted to Islam when she was twenty. Some forty years later, after a noted academic career, she travels all over the world to support processes of emancipation in the Muslim world – specifically on issues related to gender inequality.*

*"But I don't only talk about women", she tells me as we're sitting in a hotel in Brussels. She was visiting the capital of Europe to lecture during a three-day conference on LGBT in Islam. "I'm trying to envision a sort of ethical framework of what it means to be a human being", she explains. "Most of my work is, in some way or another, related to a sort of broad 'moral thrust'. So, I've been trying to challenge age-old ideas that certain inequalities would be part of Islam in various aspects of life."*

———— ❈ ————

According to many people, the world is going downhill. In classical Arabic, so I have been told, this can be expressed by the word **mounqaliba**, which could be translated as 'devolution'. But you have travelled all over the world to support many emancipatory efforts. Does this give you a

**more positive outlook on the future, or do you also fear the increasing polarizations between rich and poor, secular and religious, East and West, and so on?**

I do see some heightened emphasis on the dichotomy, but I'm much more optimistic, particularly when it comes to women's involvement in the reforms of their own lives. I've seen things come to fruition that I couldn't have imagined ten years ago. And even as there are some challenges to this positive thrust forward, I now see a greater connective force for Muslim women. And I love meeting young women who have just gotten engaged in the process because they make someone of sixty, like myself, even more hopeful that it will continue in a positive way. So, despite some of the backlash, I feel that we're on the move and that the move is inevitable because of the non-sustainability of the things we're facing. And it is becoming ever clearer to many people that gender inequality is one of those unsustainabilities of society. It's almost as if time itself has proven the mandate of gender equality.

**In what measure is Islam a force in this search for equality? Do most of the activists 'happen to be Muslim' while they get a wave of feminism going, or are they creating a specific strand of Islam?**

I think it's a combination. There are some people that strongly believe that the way to be successful is to leave Islam out of the formula. In regards to gender issues particularly, they rely on certain human rights instruments. So, there was a time where you could not have both Islam and human rights, but that was simply because nobody interrogated what Islam really means and who decides. On the other side, some people never interrogated human rights and just supposed that these texts weren't useful simply because they were constructed in the West. Over time, however, many people have come to see that there is no problem reconciling the different approaches. The two really aren't mutually exclusive at all and, in the end, you do not have to 'choose' one or the other. So there is no need to 'prefer' human rights over Islam and, therefore, throw away Islam.[58] All we should do is ask ourselves the question: "*Who* decides the way Islam should be lived?" And then we should ask: "*Why* would I not be able to question some of those authorities?"

## Would you then propose some sort of 'Islamic liberation theology'?

I myself do not use the term because, the way it manifested itself within Christianity, liberation theology was a force for those in a state of oppression. But I do not assume a state of oppression. Instead, I assume a state of misrepresentation, misinterpretation and misappropriation. So, there is nothing to be 'liberated' from. There is simply the need to reclaim the authenticity of Islam. And that's an aspect of social, political, economic and spiritual transformation.

That's why I prefer the term 'reformed theology'. This is not the same as what is often called 'liberal Islam' because 'liberal Islam' only extracts some convenient elements out of Islamic theology, as well as other articulations of human well-being, and tries to leave the rest behind. But the methodology of a 'reformed theology' explicitly looks at the entire Islamic corpus. It specifically takes the responsibility for weighing the advantageous aspects of that classical legacy while, at the same time, challenging biases and misappropriations. It will question the intellectual and philosophical roots of injustices and will question the work that is done under the pervasive patriarchal thrust of human civilisation – but *from* the sources, which means that a 'reformed theology' will make use of the Qur'an and the life of the Prophet to attack

---

[58] My conversation with Musdah Mulia, later in this book, makes this very clear. See p. 209.

aspects of misappropriation.

Let me give you a small example. As you know, I have been leading our local community in prayer. You will hear people who categorically say: "In Islam, women shouldn't lead the Muslim community in prayer." But the question must then be asked: "How do you come to those conclusions? What is your evidence?" And when you look back, you'll not only see that the Qur'an does *not* prohibit women from being imam or leading in prayer. The Qur'an also doesn't say they *have* to be male. Likewise, the Prophet *never* prohibited women from becoming an imam and never said it *had* to be a man. So, if the Qur'an and sunnah have no explicit confirmation of that opinion, we have to wonder how we came to that opinion.

The answer is that it originated out of juridical interpretation. But if the primary sources do not advocate the conclusion of the juridical interpretation – to say nothing even of the diversity of opinions within the juridical interpretations – you have the right and, in fact, even the mandate to interrogate that finding and to challenge the notion that it is or isn't Islamic.

**I once read an article of yours that put forward Aisha, the Prophet's wife, as a female example to reinterpret the gender equations in Islam. The article didn't go very far into the subject, however. Yet, to me as a Christian, it seemed like a very good idea. From within my own tradition, I'm used to having particular historical people put forward as examples of how to handle certain contemporary issues. Saint Francis is one of those examples. The Franciscan inspiration is of great importance in the Christian tradition when we're thinking about our faith's relation to ecology. Some sort of 'Aishology' would, therefore, make sense to me as an Islamic inspiration for the discussion on how to handle the equality of men and women.**

The article you refer to is called 'Aisha's legacy', but that title was given to me. I would never take a title like that myself since I have a problem with the use of precedents to 'prove' certain things. We, for example, don't have a historical precedent of a women's interpretation of the Qur'anic texts until the twentieth century, but that doesn't mean women aren't supposed to interpret the Qur'an. The difficulty for women to pursue a scholarly career had nothing to do with divine sanction but was simply a matter of logistics. As a woman alone, you could not bundle up your possessions on the back of a camel and travel to Baghdad when you had some intellectual cravings. Today, however, we have the Internet and planes and all that kind of stuff, so there is no problem anymore for anyone to go and seek knowledge, get degrees and so on. Should we then not allow women to pursue more knowledge simply because they did not do it in the past?

As such, I do not base arguments on precedent or specific examples. I simply argue on the basis of *any* example. It could be a female example that benefits men, and it could be a male example that benefits women. In my Qur'anic exegesis, I base this on the wording of the text in Surah 66 – At-Tahrim – where it says: "God has given examples of disbelievers: the wives of Noah and Lot who married two of Our righteous servants but betrayed them. Their husbands could not help them against God: it was said, 'Both of you enter the fire with the others.' God has also given examples of believers: Pharaoh's wife, who said, 'Lord, build me a house near You in the Garden. Save me from Pharaoh and his actions; save me from the evildoers,' and Mary daughter of Imran. She guarded her chastity, so We breathed into her from Our spirit. She accepted the truth from her Lord's words and Scriptures: she was truly devout."[59]

---

[59] 66:9-12 from M.A.S. Abdel Haleem, The Qur'an. A new translation, Oxford University Press, 2004, p. 381. As the expression 'so We breathed into her from Our spirit' might obviously imply Christians, the Mary referred to in the last verse is, indeed, the mother of Jesus.

In the Arabic, 'believers' and 'disbelievers' are written in the male plural because that is the only form which is inclusive. That is to say, that the male plural can refer to women as well as men. In Arabic, it is only the female plural which is exclusive and, thus, can only refer to women. That means that the examples given in this surah, even though they are all female examples, actually apply to all believers and, thus, also to men.

I am, therefore, not interested in examples that serve only a specific group of people, but I look for examples that are able to help all of us achieve human excellence and that are able to help us fulfil our purpose in this creation. If it could be reached by a human being, then their example is for all human beings who are trying to achieve that excellence.

# JIHAD

Many Christians and Westerners think that the term *jihad* refers to some sort of obligatory 'holy war' that Muslims have to wage to impose an Islamic rule all over the world. But jihad, in fact, simply means 'striving'. As such, it could refer to an 'armed striving' to win a defensive battle, but it can just as well refer to the inner striving of a believer to become a better human being. A hadith explains this all too well. When the companions of the Prophet returned after a victorious battle, showing their pride and contentment, he told them: "You bring glad tidings, but you have only returned from the lesser jihad to the Greater Jihad. For the Greater Jihad is the striving of a servant of Allah against his desires."

Jihad is mainly a spiritual term, therefore, and even when it is used in a more 'worldly' sense of armed struggle, the Qur'an and the hadith – and, thus, the position of the early jurists and theologians as well – are quite clear on the matter: violence is only justified as a means of self-defence. This obviously included the defence of one's own religion. That is to say, if others forcefully try to prevent you from being a Muslim, Islam justifies resistance to this oppression and, if necessary, even by use of protective violence.

The original idea of armed jihad, therefore, entailed several conditions: the goal had to be defensive instead of aggressive; women, children and elderly should not to be harmed or killed; the natural surroundings should not be destroyed, etc.

All in all, these conditions are very congruent with the classical Catholic Just War Theory, of which the Christian scholar, Saint Thomas Aquinas, laid the grounds some six centuries later, basing himself on teachings of the Church Father, Saint Augustine of Hippo. Classical Islam and Christianity, therefore, do not differ much on this topic.

———— ❁ ————

Needless to say, theory and practice did and do not always coincide. The spread of Islam has certainly seen many wars and violent tribulations that certainly weren't merely defensive. Islamic empires have often been very combative. The Ottomans, for example, once stood at the gates of Vienna because of their desire to conquer, etching a collective panic in the European memory. And today as well, particular groups interpret the concept of jihad in a very different manner, thereby legitimizing expansionist violence on religious grounds.

Yet, such violence most certainly isn't an intrinsic part of Islam and there are plenty of historic counterexamples.

One of the most important counterexamples is the Prophet's tendency towards non-violence. He portrayed this very clearly in the peace treaty of Hudaybiyyah. This treaty was signed when the young Muslim community went on a peaceful pilgrimage to Mecca, even though they knew they could be massacred by the *Quraysh*[60]. The Muslim community grew much stronger in the ensuing years and might have benefitted from breaking the treaty, but the

---

[60] The Quraysh were a powerful merchant tribe that controlled Mecca (and, consequently, the access to the Ka'aba) at the time of the Prophet. Muhammad was born into the Banu Hashim clan of the Quraysh tribe. Because the leaders of the Quraysh did not accept his prophethood, conflicts arose and Muhammad had to flee to Medina. Only when the Quraysh were finally defeated could the Muslim community return to Mecca.

Prophet held on to it and eventually it was broken by the Meccan allies.

Another example that is very counterintuitive to the Western idea of Islam is the historic fact that the great majority of the spread of Islam was actually done through preaching and not through violence. The acquisition of lands during the rule of the majority of the caliphates was most often just that: expansion of territory. And during that expansion, Jews and Christians were seldom obliged or forced to convert.

The *Millet system* in the Ottoman Empire, for example, gave a specific status and protection to different religious communities, such as Christians and Jews. They were even allowed to use their own systems of law in particular matters. Sure, they had to pay specific taxes and sure, it wasn't complete equality, but when placed within its timeframe and context, the level of tolerance the Muslim world showed towards other religious communities was enormous and the Christian world completely shrivelled in comparison.

———— ❁ ————

Muslims aren't just a bunch of irrational bearded men who loudly shout "Allahu Akbar!" ("God is the greatest!") before they eagerly attack the 'non-believers'. For many centuries and up until today, the Western world might have presented them that way, but we only need to look at someone like Abdal Ghaffar Khan to gain a completely different image. He was a Muslim and close associate of Mahatma Gandhi. In fact, he was often called 'the Gandhi of the frontier', for this imposing man was trying to spread the message of non-violence among his Pathan community. This community lived in the frontier regions of colonial British India, which is now known as Pakistan and Afghanistan.

What Abdal Ghaffar Khan has in common with the Taliban who roam his birth region today, is the fact that he was a jihadi. But in stark contrast with those Taliban, he was a nonviolent jihadi. Just like his mentor, he called himself a soldier of peace. That is to say, he always had peace on his mind, but he was strong and courageous in his struggles as he continuously strove for justice. Even more so, he eventually created a group of one hundred thousand nonviolent soldiers. Thus, his movement of 'Khudai Khidmatgar' ('*Servants of God*') became the very first nonviolent army in history.

----------- ❁ -----------

The simple fact of the matter is that many religions contain elements of opposition and some sort of jihad against injustice. Many of the Jewish prophets were prophets exactly because they fiercely called for societal change. Even Jesus whipped the merchants out of the temple.

Cyrus McGoldrick called it 'righteous anger'. And such 'righteous anger' is also what drives many of the migrant Muslim youngsters in bigger Western cities. Their experience of discrimination, racism and non-acceptance makes them socially and politically active. A small minority call for a violent jihad, but the great bulk of the disgruntled youth strives towards more justice in a completely nonviolent manner. Sadly enough, their activism isn't always comprehended by the majority of the host society. The art and socio-political expressions they bring along often comes across as aggressive to those who don't belong to their communities; yet, those willing to listen can easily hear a genuine plea for honesty and a sincere effort to breach out of conformity – both the conformity of their own community and that of the larger society. The Islamic punk of Aki Nawaz is a perfect example thereof.

*Photo by Irna Qureshi*

# AKI NAWAZ
## ON RELIGIOUS, SOCIAL
## AND POLITICAL HONESTY

*Aki Nawaz is the front man of Fun>Da>Mental. The band often aroused controversy, not in the least for songs like 'Che Bin', which compares Osama Bin Laden to Che Guevara, or 'Cookbook DIY', which describes in detail how to make a homemade bomb. It eventually made the British press label Fun>Da>Mental as 'the Asian Public Enemy'.*

*But Aki Nawaz certainly isn't glorifying terrorism. If anything, he simply tries to breach all stereotypes to stir debate. For years, he has been criticizing narrow thinking, challenging societal convictions and addressing the politics of racism. His quite undefinable style of music, which sometimes mixes qawwali with hip hop or puts Qur'an verses underneath some industrial rock, always add to the message.*

---- ❁ ----

**You've been an outspoken voice for several decades now, through your music as well as through activism and public discussion. But after all these years, aren't you getting fed up with it? Don't you feel that it all constantly repeats itself and that all the talk about a possible clash of cultures eventually creates a self-fulfilling prophecy?**

It's definitely not the discussion I'm fed up with. I love discussion. I'm fed up with the lack of discussion. There are so many nuances, layers and characters that are never heard.

I've been in Gaza, I've spoken to jihadists, I've made documentaries about Guantanamo, I've travelled the Middle East . . . There are so many different positions, there is so much conflict, so much pain and so much suffering that needs understanding. And, in all of this, context is one of the biggest casualties. Many people simply don't place things in perspective and make simple dichotomous caricatures of others.

It's very hard to bring context and nuance back into the debate because we don't have the correct platform to discuss or challenge the mainstream ideas. Islam is on the back foot to articulate itself because we only get twenty seconds to discuss things on the existing platforms. As a result, we forget how to build bridges and became very good at burning them.

**But isn't that partly the way you work? For example, when you wrote 'Cookbook DIY', you could have known what the reaction of the public would have been – two members of the parliament of the United Kingdom even called for your arrest. Not a lot of people would spontaneously see that as a way to build bridges, but rather as something that would burn them.**

Well, it is, but at the same time, it isn't. You can listen to the first, the second or the third verse. We knew they'd present the first verse. But they completely and utterly missed the point, because if you listen to all of it and look at the video, you'll see a Christian jihadist. They interpreted it as a Muslim jihadist when it wasn't.

Our intention was to challenge the ideas that had been put forward. Music can only do that up to a certain extent. So, we thought we'd challenge it on many fronts. Of course, we knew it would lead to confusion, but the confusion was already there because they're calling *me* a terrorist while I know *they* are terrorists.

So, what gives them the dominating attitude to dictate the parameters?

One of the aspects I actually like about the West is that they respect eccentricity, eclecticism and individualism. They respect these things a bit more than many contemporary Muslim cultures. I think that's great. But, nowadays, they only want those things for themselves and not for me. Where does the audacity come from to even consider this position of superiority? I've travelled to South Africa and I've been to colonial countries. I know what the Europeans did everywhere. Somebody should tell them their own history and explain to them what they did.

I really want to be a bridge builder, but I also don't want to be dictated to. My bridge building bears on equality, mutual respect and understanding. Because I've taken that perspective, it pushes me away from a lot of Muslim groups, while those at the other end – the secular, liberal or whatever you want to call them – think I'm too Islamic.

**When I discovered your music many years ago, Islam didn't seem to be much at the forefront of your music. Have you always had that religious sentiment?**

I had it, but I didn't know I had it. I used to talk about racism. It worked for everybody. They all understood what you were saying. We didn't have to talk about something like hijabs for one, because there were hardly any around when we were growing up. But now we're pushed against the wall because of our religion.

So what place am I fighting for these days? Do I want to compromise with religious people who I find very blinded and indoctrinated? I don't, because I've seen the horrible things that such people have done. I don't want to be a part of that. But I also don't want to be a part of the other lot. They're all indoctrinated, the jihadi in his jihadism, the neoliberal in his neoliberalism. So, I am very happy being absolutely, completely and utterly independent.

My first ever love for Islam was when I read in the Qur'an 'blessed are the rebels with righteous cause and faith'. That's the way I look at Islam and that's the way I'm going to stay, because I'm not going to buy the indoctrination of my parents' culture nor the indoctrination of the secularists.

**And how do you, someone who makes crossover hip hop punk, relate to the Prophet?**

The Prophet was a dignified human being with all the problems and the issues of the concepts of his time. Although, I do have a few problems with some hadith. I don't deny them but, in these matters as well, I'm completely opposed to not having the platform to discuss them. I can believe the Qur'an when I read its verses, but I have a problem believing in the Qur'an because I *have* to.

We need to debate many hadiths and passages of the Qur'an because I don't believe Islam is part of a timeline. I think it's something that reinvents itself with context. We don't have an institute – which is fabulous – but we lack leadership and leftist politics in Islam.

That's why I wanted Osama Bin Laden to be somebody who could see the whole picture, but he didn't, just like most other jihadists. There should be a certain nobleness in jihad. Yet, after all the people I've met, it became clear to me that out of a hundred fighters, there's maybe ten or fifteen people who are actually noble, dignified and decent in their hearts. Most of the others are just like the English here. They don't have the spirit of true resistance. Neither do they have the spirit of humbleness or mercy. They forget that the Qur'an only allows defending yourself, but not transgressing. People like Osama Bin Laden don't realize the limits of transgression. Had he done that, there might have been a real shift. But when Al Qaeda looks at the world now, what did it achieve? More Muslims have been killed and there's more resentment. It has been magnified. The response of the West as well. So now there are two terrorists: the Muslim terrorists and the West.

**I come back to my previous question then. Do you think your way of igniting things even more with your choice of music and words is a step forward in mending some of these issues?**

You know, it goes back to my punk days. It is stating: "Don't force parameters on me that you're already used to. Don't tell me I can't be eccentric."

**But is it effective? Does such a type of 'f*** you! statement' win over people?**

It's true. I will sometimes say and do things just to test and see what the reaction will be. Perhaps there's a perverted logic to it, but dissent is a very bizarre tool and it's simply a part of my character.

I think, however, that there's something fundamentally wrong with the human psyche and the current thought process – and it might just be because we're all at each other. I can't handle this 'right wing' and 'left wing', for example. I see the right and I see chaos. And I see the left and I think: "Be true to it." Because when they come into power they say the same things the right does. I actually believe that people really want to see socialism work in a good way, but they don't make it work. And in all of this chaos, human beings are simply becoming a currency.

**One of my teachers once drew my attention to the awfulness of the concept of 'human resources' – if you really look at it, you can see that it means that in contemporary economics, humans have been degraded to resources.**

That's what I'm saying. My children's children are going to become a spiritless currency. It's pretty fucking sad.

You know, I don't have anything against money or capitalism because capitalism really doesn't need to create all the chaos it creates at the moment. What it could do is make everybody valuable. If you want to be a monster eating money, then you should give houses to families, jobs to people and make them more valuable because then they can spend, spend, spend and buy your products. So, even the capitalists aren't consistent.

I just see so much corruption and bad motives everywhere – also within our own Muslim communities.

**Certainly so, but at the same time, I also have a lot of hope for the world. The economic globalism does produce a lot of injustices, but exactly because of globalism, it also becomes impossible to simply hold on to one single view. It's the same for the friction between secularism and Islam: whatever painful situations it creates at the moment, at least, step by step, it becomes totally impossible to hold on to one single secular and neo-liberal concept of the future.**

We'll see . . . When we did the song, 'I reject', the only line that people picked up and made a fuss about was: 'I reject your mini-skirt liberation'. But they failed to grasp that the line actually comes from the women's liberation movement *in England!* Only twenty or thirty years ago, those women went out, sprayed graffiti and bombed sex shops. So, that's why they shouted to males how they rejected such a 'sexual liberation' that wasn't one. And they were right. But, I'm Muslim, so I got it on my head when I used the same sentence.

# IJTIHAD

The Islamic tradition knows a long lasting debate about the precise balance between personal interpretation, scholarly advice and the authority of revelation. Some groups placed extreme emphasis on revelation and denounced 'normal humans' capacity to go beyond the teachings that were revealed to mankind through the prophets. Other groups transferred all authority to the scholars when they had received the proper educational backgrounds to advance particular insights. Still other groups focussed very heavily on rational reflection, sometimes even up to the point that they saw revelation as an unnecessary addition to religion.

This shouldn't be all too difficult to grasp from a Christian perspective. The very split between Protestantism and Catholicism was brought about along very similar lines. Much of the discussions during the reformation and counter-reformation revolved around the tensions between the different views on the place of the Bible, the authority of the clerisy (or papacy) and the spiritual self-reliance of the faithful individual.

That's also why Christians should be able to understand that, even though such philosophical tensions might often come up and sometimes create certain extremes, this doesn't make the tradition as a whole narrow-minded. Considered from a broader historical perspective, the Christian traditions did recognize a balance between the elements of revelation, scholarship and personal interpretation. The same is most certainly true for Islam as well. To varying degrees, therefore, personal reflection has always had its place within Islam. Besides the Qur'an and the teachings of the Ulama and in varying degrees, there always was a place for a process of personal theological and spiritual interpretation. This process is called *ijtihad*.

Today, however, one can often hear that the 'bap al ijtihad' is closed – that is to say, 'that the gates of personal interpretation' are closed. Yet, unlike what many might think, this wasn't some sort of fatwa brought up by literalist and traditionalist religious authorities. In fact, the texts discussing this 'closure of the gates of interpretation' do not bring it up as a ruling, but rather as a matter of fact. After centuries of debate and discussion, many scholars had the feeling that most issues had been handled and that little extra intellectual advancement was or could be needed. Thus, they didn't say that interpretation wasn't allowed; they simply thought there was little need for it.

Such reasoning is actually quite reminiscent of the manner in which a Western scholar could write an applauded treatise titled *The End of History*, in which the current Western socio-political model was described as a final stage of human social and intellectual development. "What we may be witnessing is not just the end of the Cold War or the passing of a particular period of post-war history, but the end of history as such." Fukuyama wrote in 1992, "It's the end point of mankind's ideological evolution and the universalization of Western liberal democracy as the final form of human government."

Much rethinking of Western values and core ideologies did not seem necessary to the many academics that followed this thesis. And even though this idea of socio-political finality was also frequently criticized, in much of the mainstream depictions of our current world, the Western modernist model of neoliberal and nation-state-based democracy was and still is presented as the final pinnacle of civilisation that should eventually be implemented everywhere.

But, we certainly haven't reached the end of history. Reinterpretation is happening in the West as well as the East. Whether we're talking about Christianity, modernity or Islam, in the end, ijtihad simply can't be held back.

No matter how much certain rulers of Islamic countries might try, completely muffling dissent turns out to be an impossible task. Precisely because the Ummah has no single centre, not only authority but also critique can come from every corner. So, although the traditional scholars still receive a great deal of respect, a whole new layer of activists, artists and intellectuals has stood up as well. In various ways and often in a very personal style, they do not only confront the injustices within their own community; they also attack the modernist dogmas of today's globalized neoliberal culture.

Ziauddin Sardar is another prominent example thereof. He's a man who receives much appreciation and support because of his critical and very independent interpretations, but he's also often critiqued for his untraditional stances. As such, some groups and scholars will sometimes attack him because he's not a classical scholar, but classical or not, he has been and still is an important intellectual who has played an active role in several projects that stirred innovating discussions and debates.

# ZIAUDDIN SARDAR
## ON CRITICAL MUSLIMS AND
## TRANSMODERN TRADITION

*In his distinctly personal and independent style, Ziauddin Sardar wrote over
45 books, guest blogged in the Guardian and presented a number of programs
for the BBC and Channel 4.*

*For many decades, this polymath has portrayed a relentless intellectual energy.
The titles of his books varied from 'The Future of Muslim Civilisation' to
'Why Do People Hate America?' to 'The A to Z of Postmodern Life', and
his professional life includes periods of research work for the Hajj Research
Centre in the 1970s and an advisory position in the cabinet of Anwar
Ibrahim, the former Deputy Prime Minister of Malaysia in the late 1980s.*

*When I met this somewhat fidgety but very welcoming man in London, his
main preoccupation was editorial work for the intellectual magazines 'Critical
Muslim' and 'East West Affairs'. The former bundles contemporary Muslim
ideas and thought, the latter is a journal of North-South relations in
postnormal times.*

———— ❁ ————

You are known as an outspoken critic of tradition. Yet, my
own 'journey through Islam' has, in fact, rekindled a great
deal of my respect for traditions – both the Islamic tradition

**as well as my own Christian tradition.**

Traditions carry much beauty within themselves, but a great many problems also come from tradition. Normally, traditions are not something static. They are constantly reinvented, so to say. In fact, a tradition stays a tradition by reinventing itself. If it doesn't reinvent itself, it can become a custom and a custom can become very oppressive. And a great part of the contemporary problem is that much of our tradition is ossified, frozen in history, very misogynist and has a great fear of 'the other'. On top of it, certain aspects of these ossified traditions are very deathly, such as not allowing free thought, killing apostates or like traditions that are oppressive towards sexual orientation.

Many of these traditions actually come from what I would call 'manufactured hadiths'. Therefore, all criticism has to start with our own sources. We should never accept all the hadiths that are thrown at us, without critically engaging with them.

**Is it not so, however, that the Islamic tradition normally does critically engage with them, for example, by trying to find the chain of narrators in order to figure out the authority of a certain hadith?**

Sure, but we have to keep in mind that the methodologies have moved on. There are new ways of criticizing. Even within the old traditional methodologies, I do not think that the hadith criticism was good enough. Two of the premises of accepting a hadith are that it shouldn't contradict the Qur'an and that it should be a rational hadith, yet lots of accepted hadiths do, in fact, contradict the Qur'an and are totally irrational. According to Bukhari, for example, one hadith explains, "Seeing a black woman in a dream is the sign of an oncoming epidemic." Or what are we to make of the hadith from *The Book of Nikah* that tells us, "The Messenger used to visit all nine of his wives every night." How could any man, no matter how close he was to the Prophet, have known this? And even if some men might know more about his nocturnal relationships with his wives, how could he humanly have done that, particularly when we are told elsewhere in the same collection that he used to pray all night, so much so that his feet swelled?

We can say the same about Qur'an interpretation. We have the classical Qur'anic methodology that we have to interpret the Qur'an from within the Qur'an, where we have to look at the historical context, and so on. But even that has not really been followed. Some of the classical commentaries, thus, are pretty irrational and unreasonable in terms of what they say about women, about Christians or the way they speak about belief.

**Obviously, I agree that both Muslims and Christians should critically engage with their sources — certainly when traditional interpretations gave rise to certain discriminatory or suppressive situations. Yet, on the other hand, belief can never be a totally 'rational' or 'reasonable' concept. You can't be endlessly critical and analytic about it, I would say. It is, in the end, also a matter of 'acceptance'.**

Belief certainly doesn't have to be a totally rational thing. There is such a thing as 'a leap of faith'. But the leap of faith is about God. In a sense, God has to remain the unseen. Because if God can be seen or if you can prove him by logical argument, everybody will believe in God and there will be no need for faith. What follows after the leap of faith, however, has to be based on some notion of rationality, objectivity, analysis and method. We can't just believe something because people tell us they found it in the Qur'an or because they heard a particular hadith.

That's why criticism is so important. Actually, for me, the greatness of the Muslim civilisation resides in its criticism. The early Muslim scholars were very critical, even those who canonized Islamic law. And they expected that those who would follow them would be equally critical. The whole idea of the hadith collection, for example, was based on criticism, but the generations that followed them did not pay much attention to this aspect of criticism and a lot more to following their predecessors. One person follows the previous one, and he, in turn, is followed by another, so there's rather a chain of followers instead of critical engagement with the text.

**And, of course, many feminist Muslim scholars have pointed out that most of the Qur'an and hadith interpretations were done by men and, as such, many of those interpretations have been far too patriarchal.**

They're absolutely correct on this. Even more so, they weren't just men, but men with a very tribal outlook on life so that their tribal culture became a part of the *tafsir*[61] and the manufacturing of hadiths.

So, without a critical engagement with our sources, I don't think we have much of a future. This blind faith on tradition is absolutely appalling.

But – and this is an emphasized 'but' – I do understand that you cannot ditch tradition completely. You do need traditions. They are very important for our sanity because they give us a sense of identity and purpose in life. Actually, this is where criticism comes in – or positive criticism at least. Negative criticism simply deconstructs and destroys. But positive criticism tries to take us forward. Positive criticism tries to preserve and promote the many life-enhancing elements of our traditions.

**Nowadays, many people will turn to what they call the 'Sufi tradition' to find such life-enhancing elements of Islam. Throughout my many conversations, I got a more nuanced**

---

[61] Tafsir is the explanatory interpretations of Qur'anic verses.

**view on this matter, but how do you assess this quite modern focus on 'Sufism'?**

Lots of people are often impressed by Sufi teachings and Sufi talk on tradition, but Sufis themselves have contributed a great deal to misogynist and authoritarian thought in Muslim culture. In classical Sufi tariqas, for example, you're often supposed to accept your shaykh unquestioningly. But why? Is he God? Why should I accept anyone unquestioningly? Of course I should *learn* from the shaykh, but I should be able to discuss, debate and openly criticize when I deem it necessary. I find this whole idea of a 'guru' and 'disciple' quite repugnant. Lots of Sufi's are, however, promoting such things.

Exactly the same methodology is used by groups like Al Qaeda, by the way. In those circles, you're also not supposed to question the authority.

All of that Sufi business is often just recycling the old traditional stuff. Now, I don't mind that people engage with great minds like Ibn Arabi or Rumi and their illuminating thought. What I dislike is the uncritical perpetuation of certain traditional elements.

**Can we really compare this type of historic ossification to the current trend of Salafi-style ossification of Islam?**

The underlying process is the same. First of all it involves an exaggerated 'reverence'. It's about giving complete reverence to authorities, teachers or your shaykhs and idealizing them as perfect human beings who can solve all problems. This comes with a fear of failure. In the presence of such an idealized figure, you are afraid to be wrong because it feels like a sin. But, of course, questioning and criticism necessarily involves getting it wrong. *Being human* means that you sometimes make mistakes. If you're perfect, you won't, but if you're human, you will.

So fear, idealization and over-reverence are essential in this matter, and they're nothing new. The fourteenth century Ibn Khaldun criticized others for exactly these three things.

**Today, however, these things are also strongly connected to specific economic and political realities, the spread of Petro-Islam from the Gulf being one of them.**

I think the Gulf and the Saudi's have done a lot to promote *Wahhabism*[62] and closing the minds of Muslims. But that's hardly surprising. It's a very tribal society. In fact, their construction of God is a bit like the leader of the Quraysh. He's always angry, he's always vengeful and he's always protective of his tribe. The whole 'image' they made of God is, therefore, very problematic in my eyes. Where's the mercy? Where's the beauty? Where's humanity? If you look at God's 99 names, those aspects are among them as well, yet they tend to ignore them.

**When I spoke to Dr. D. Latifa, she said: "Their work is done. They've created the priests, now they will claim Mecca as the Rome of Islam."**

She was right. They act quite like an empire and it's painful to see how they're transforming Mecca very much into a city like imperial Rome. All the cultural property has been removed. They build huge hotels, shopping malls and palaces right behind the Great Mosque. It's not much of a sacred city anymore. It's a pretty ugly city in many respects. Of course, the Kaaba and its surroundings will always be sacred to Muslims, but once you go outside of it, you're greeted with much ugliness.

**Your criticism of such issues is very outspoken and**

---

[62] A particular form of Salafism. It bases itself on the teachings of Muhammad Ibn Abdal Wahhab. It eventually became the official ideology of the Saudi state. Wahhabis do not like the term 'Wahhabism' and, instead, will simply call themselves Salafis or Muwahhidun, the latter meaning 'unitarians'.

**straightforward. Often, that type of criticism evokes a counter reaction that pushes people outside the community. Do you sometimes have the feeling you're being pushed outside the Muslim community?**

Of course people sometimes get upset by my criticism, but fortunately, I'm still seen as part of the community and I still see myself as a part of it. And what is a community in any case? You can create community in various ways. There's also a community of critical Muslims, for example. Yet, criticism is frowned upon everywhere. It's not a specific Muslim problem. If you're American and criticize America, for example, you'll experience the same thing. Those in power always despise criticism. But those in power can also only be held accountable through criticism. So criticism is essential to accountability.

**The possibility to hold things accountable seems to diminish, however, as we witness a worldwide growth of narrow-minded conservatism that increasingly restricts freedom of thought and action.**

I think this growth of conservatism is produced by fear. When people fear change, they look inwards and try to create boundaries. A big part of the problem for conservatives has been the accelerating rate of change. Look at computers; their computing power doubles every six months, so to speak. It took thirty years to take the first genome out of a fly and now we can take genomes out of everything in a matter of days. How we approach the body, what we regard as life, how we need to construct society, and so on — all these things have become major issues. As a result, people come together and focus on their particular group, creating 'us versus them' boundaries in their effort to navigate the sea of change. Of course, fear of the others was already there, but when you bring in rapid change, it increases manifold and uncertainty becomes dominant. And people who want certainty often find it in certain literal notions of religion. They simplify things and make clear cut lists of dos and don'ts. Yet, this only creates an illusion of certainty, because, in the end, there is no ultimate certainty.

**Postmodern philosophy starts from exactly this premise, that there aren't any ultimate certainties in lives. Nonetheless, besides being an outspoken critic of ossified Islamic traditions, you're also a critic of modernism and postmodernism. You've written several texts and books on the matter. In a sense, I see great similarities between the two topics of critique, because modernity as it exists today, is, in my eyes, also an ossification, but then of the secular, atheistic, scientific idea that all value can eventually be levelled down to the preferences of the individual. You wrote about the need for 'transmodernity' in this respect. What do you exactly mean by it?**

As you say, we know that there are lots of problems with modernism. Postmodernism is supposed to critique modernity and take us forward. But it has turned out to be a new form of Western imperialism. Everything is vanity, there are no ground narratives, nothing gives meaning, there is no sense of direction, etc. These postmodern 'building blocks' are absolutely untrue; they only have us staring in a void. So, we need to go beyond them. That's where transmodernity comes in.

Transmodernity is an effort to go beyond modernity and postmodernity. We need to bring the life-enhancing aspects of tradition and the best aspects of modernity together. They need to be synthesized into a new way of looking at things. In modernity, tradition is always looked down upon. In transmodernity, tradition is critiqued, but then the best bits of tradition are kept and built upon. In postmodernism, modernism is almost seen as evil. But again, in transmodernity, modernity is critiqued and its best aspects are enhanced. So, it's a much more critically engaging process that takes the best of what was already there. It doesn't disconnect you from history, but builds upon elements that can take you forward.

## What are some of the most valuable aspects of tradition which, in your eyes, the world needs today?

The whole idea of family as a basic unit on which the community and society is built is a good example. Or the way in which traditional societies have engaged with nature. They don't see nature as something that needs to be conquered. Nature, to them, is something that you work and live with. So, if traditional societies are allowed to follow their traditions, they tend to be ecologically sound. Look at Fez in Morocco, for example. It's built along a river, but in such a way that the water is not polluted as it flows downstream. Traditionally, they also allowed certain parts outside the city to be 'haram' so that people could not cut the trees of the woodlands.

The tragedy of the Islamic tradition is that we've lost the positive life-enhancing aspects of it. Sadly enough, we trap ourselves in those aspects of tradition that are often deathly.

## So what does the future have in store for us?

Given the global trends, I believe that all too narrow-minded thought will become obsolete. It can, of course, do much damage in the short run, but in the long run, the fundamentalist and literalist rhetoric will eventually prove itself to be totally insufficient and disappear. There will always be fundamentalists and literalists – in fact, we need them in order to have a complete human society with all shades of opinion – but they will not be dominant. They will lose their engine. The engine at the moment is Saudi Arabia. And the engine will only be running as long as the oil is flowing — not much longer in other words. Therefore, Muslim fundamentalism doesn't have much of a future. It's just a bunch of slogans without many pragmatic solutions. It's the people who produce pragmatic solutions who will eventually win the day.

**Quite an optimistic outlook for a continuously critical person like you.**

A religious person has to be optimistic by nature, because religion is all about hope.

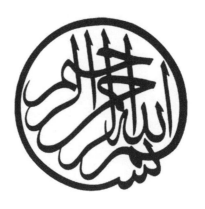

# TRANSCENDING
# THE TENSION

# TAWHID

One of the core concepts of Islam is the belief that there is only one God and that this God is not divided within Himself. Initially, everything comes from Him and eventually everything returns to Him. But even though he can be witnessed, perceived and even experienced within all that exists, his unique transcendence ultimately remains untouched by the coming and passing of every piece of creation. This is called *tawhid*.

The strong emphasis on the oneness of God forms a stark contrast, however, with the plurality and diversity of the Muslim community. As I have already explained in the chapter on sharia, the real unity of the Ummah lies in its diversity.

Sadly enough, this 'unity in diversity' hasn't always been taken for granted. Although it's a strong principle of Islam, the history of the Islamic world has witnessed much sectarian conflict. Even more so, the persecution of other Muslims has often been far greater than the violence inflicted on those who held different beliefs and adhered to different faiths.

Nevertheless, even though certain Muslim communities started to see themselves as religiously more pure or politically more important than others, in the end, none of them has ever been able to dominate all other groups or unilaterally impose its very own interpretation and style.

As Dr. Latifa explained, the present day far-reaching Arabisation of the Muslim world is quite a painful anomaly since the cultural, political and social diversity of Islam has by and large been quite enormous.

Westerners tend to forget, for example, that only 15% of Muslims worldwide are Arabs, while the biggest majority Muslim country is actually Indonesia. Even more so, the sum of Indonesian and Indian Muslims accounts for a bigger percentage of the worldwide Muslim population than all others combined. And let it be clear that the traditional Islam in Indonesia or India is enormously different from the cultural expressions of Islam in the Gulf or Middle East.

Yet, much of the other cultural expressions are rapidly being eroded in many regions of the Muslim world as they are caught in the maelstrom of geo-politics and globalised economics. As already explained in the first chapters and as my conversation with Ziauddin Sardar made quite clear once more, these tensions are predominantly a messy dialectic between the global consumption culture of modernity and the need to retain or rekindle old traditions. Instead of finding life enhancing ways to combine modernity and tradition, it often ends up in a clash between the two, which creates extremes on both sides. Thus, the neoliberal, hedonistic consumption society, as well as the aggressive, rigorous forms of Islam, ruin much of the century old cultural and spiritual diversity.

This, of course, is not a problem that only befalls the Muslim world. Muslims simply find themselves at the forefront of it all. Luckily, many people also succeed in transcending these tensions.

Perhaps this is even what binds all my conversations together: they show the possibility of finding an inspiring balance between solid tradition and globalised modernity. For, all in their own way, the people I was blessed to meet succeed in combining a thorough focus on the tawhid of the divine with a genuine acceptance of the diversity of humanity.

The Indonesian, Musdah Mulia, and her views on human rights portray this yet again.

# MUSDAH MULIA
## ON DIVINE HUMAN RIGHTS

*Musdah Mulia is one of those scholars who relentlessly combines activism, politics and academia. She has been Senior Advisor of the Minister of Religious Affairs of the Republic of Indonesia and Head of the Research Division of The Council of Indonesian Ulama. She regularly lectures at both Indonesian and international universities. Currently, much of her attention goes to the Indonesian Conference on Religion for Peace, an independent organization dedicated to advancing and promoting interfaith dialogue, democracy and peace in Indonesia.*

*Musdah's direct experience with the social and political discrimination of women in Indonesia has always given her work a strong focus on human rights and gender equality. In 2004, for example, she was the coordinator of the state endorsed Gender Mainstreaming Team. The eventual results of the team's research weren't easily accepted as many factions deemed them too liberal. Nevertheless, Musdah's approach can also count on much support from Indonesian, as well as international, circles of Muslim scholars.*

———— ✿ ————

**People often forget that Indonesia is the country with the highest population of Muslims in the world, even though it's not an Islamic state.**

Indeed. Eighty-five per cent of the Indonesian population is

Muslim, but our founding fathers and mothers didn't make Islam the state ideology. They realized that there are too many differences in interpretation, so they settled on the *Pancasila* instead. This Pancasila is a combination of five general principles that could create a common ground: spirituality, humanity, unity of the country, democracy and justice. As such, Islam isn't the sole basis of our governance, but the Pancasila incorporates many of its values because when you talk about the principle of spirituality, you talk about a spirituality that touches on love, compassion and mercy. You talk about a spirituality that goes to the essence of all faiths and religions.

**Yet, although the Pancasila offers a lot of room to build a spiritual society, sadly enough this does not seem to suffice for some more radical groups that would like to implement a purely Islamic political order.**

Sure, Indonesia has its fair share of reactionary groups. Yet, we must be aware of the fact that the rise of more radical groups coincides with the advent of democracy. As everybody knows, the Suharto regime was a very repressive regime, but once it fell and democracy found its way, it was also used and abused by radical Islamic groups. In the Suharto era, they would simply have been repressed, but now they are given the public space to spread their views. So yes, many Muslim leaders – and certainly feminist Muslims like me – are faced with the growth of radicalism.

We have to keep in mind, however, that the expressions of religious radicalism – like disadvantaging women in the Muslim community – come from the religious interpretation of those who possess the religious authority. It doesn't stem from religion itself. So, the solution to the problem, ironically enough, lies in countering them with the 'democracy' of our own religion; that is to say, with ijtihad, the process of constantly (re)interpreting our religion. Ijtihad means that we search for new ways to properly apply our religion within our contemporary contexts. With proper ijtihad then, we can explain to people that the goal of upholding human rights is not only in accordance with the Pancasila but also with the teachings of Islam

**How, then, do you counter the arguments of certain Muslim groups that consider the idea of human rights to be non-Islamic?**

Many Muslims see human rights as set of Western values. They perceive it as an ideological framework that's being forced upon them. However, they forget that, in the twelfth century, the great scholar, Al Ghazali, already said that the *maqasid al-sharia*[63] can be formulated into five basic rights of a human being that should be provided for by religion. In my view, he talks about five human rights and, more precisely, about the right to life, the right to religious freedom, the right to express your opinion freely, the right to property and the right to reproduction.

Like Al Ghazali, I strongly believe that religion came to us for the betterment of human kind, not for the betterment of God. God has no defects or problems. So, it's not God who 'needs' religion. It's humans who need it.

**But if you build your argument on tradition and even refer to Al Ghazali, why then does it often remain difficult to convince people of the 'Islamicness' of your approach to human rights?**

Sadly enough, the religious interpretation being spread and taught in our cities is the conservative interpretation. That is why I try to let people read the Qur'an and try to help them understand their religious teachings. Only when you take enough time to educate

---

[63] The Maqasid al Sharia are the 'intentions of the Sharia'. That is to say, they are the underlying purpose behind the Islamic laws.

everyone, can they come to understand that there is no contradiction between Islam and human rights values and that there is no contradiction between tawhid and democracy.

**In itself, the spiritual principle of tawhid refers to both the unity and the uniqueness of God. So, how exactly do you connect it to democracy?**

As you know, every Muslim accepts the principle of tawhid. In its essence, tawhid is the unity of God as it is expressed in our creed of faith: there is no God except THE God. A direct result of this tawhid is the fact that no creature can be equal to God, and the conviction that no human equals God gives rise to the principle of the equality of humankind. For a king cannot be a god to his people, a husband cannot be a god to his wife, a man cannot be a god to a woman, etc. Because no one is a god, no human can be superior to another human. All are fundamentally equal. No one can decree his will to someone else as if he was God.

From this, obviously, follows that all forms of discrimination against women or minorities can be considered as a denial of the principle of tawhid. A true understanding of tawhid seeks the liberation of all human beings from every form of tyranny, dictatorship or despotic structure. A true understanding of tawhid and Islam should bring about a society based on moral, civil and humanitarian values that frees it from any injustice or suppression.

**In your work, you have a strong focus on the empowerment of women. I suppose, then, that the principle of tawhid is the driving force behind it as well.**

Indeed. Women have to realize that they are full human beings with basic rights. They think they are the 'second' human being, created from Adam. It makes them feel as if they aren't 'complete' human beings, but the Qur'an doesn't say that Eve is created out of Adam's rib. That idea comes from the Bible. Yet, when our religious leaders speak – both male and female – they mention that rib. Women should learn that in the Qur'an we come from the same essence, that both male and female are called to stewardship of creation. In the eyes of God, both men and women have the same obligation to build a civil society and to work towards peace with ourselves, others and the whole of creation.

Sadly enough, however, we don't find such ideas in our current socio-political system. Many of the current articles in Indonesian common law marginalize and discriminate women. This inequality has deep roots within the patriarchal culture of our country and has pervaded our juridical system. It influences the decision-making processes of our prosecutors and judges.

**So, how do you confront these deeply embedded imbalances as a woman?**

To breach the social and political patriarchy, we need a cultural reconstruction, which should rest on three pillars. First of all, we need to have more education, in schools certainly but also in family life. Because it's above all in family life that people should raise their kids with a critical and open mind. Second, we need to change laws and regulations and we need to get rid of the subordination of women in family law. And third, we need a reinterpretation of religion so that it becomes compatible with humanity and human rights.

And let me be clear that these things aren't only necessary in Muslim communities. Christian and Hindu women face similar problems. We are all in the same boat. We all need a humanistic reinterpretation of our religions.

**Do your efforts of reinterpretation bring you into much conflict with other scholars?**

Some conservatives actually agree that the things I propose are truthful and just, but that our society isn't ready for them yet. Other women aren't educated like I am, they say. Even my husband doesn't like that I provoke people with humanistic progressive interpretations of Islam. *(Musdah laughs.)* But when people tell me: "Musdah, you're so ambitious", I readily answer: "I'm not ambitious. It's simply my right."

**And even ambition is your right, I would say. The Islamic tradition knows a lot of powerful women. The stories surrounding the wives of the Prophet, such as Khadijah and Aisha, portray this all too well.**

That's another good example of how we neglect many noble things in our religion. Nowadays, they depict Khadija as a rich widow and Aisha as a pretty wife of Muhammad, while both of them were strong women who commanded men – Khadija in her business and Aisha as the leader of an army. People easily forget what such brave women have accomplished. Much historical context got lost in our teaching of Islam. And we often don't know how to place everything within our present context and time.

Just look at the way we deal with the Qur'an. The verses in the Qur'an can actually be divided in two types: universal verses that speak of basic values to all human life and specific verses for specific contexts. Thus, when interpreting the latter they can only be understood in light of the former, i.e. the call for compassion and justice. For example, when you speak of marriage, you have to place it within bigger moral values like love and fidelity. But many scholars and preachers give too much attention to the implementation of certain contextual verses and don't place them in the context of the universal verses. This often makes their judgements and interpretations very strict, exclusive and very female unfriendly.

In the end, it's quite simple: the Qur'an comes from God, the interpretation comes from men. I'm not an infidel when I say this. And I can't stress it enough: we need to realize that the interpretation of religious truths always exists within a certain context. That is why education is so important. Education makes it possible to get rid of the dangerous and misleading forms of religion that bring about injustice and discrimination. Certainly in the case of women, they are on the back foot, socio-economically speaking. So, women have to become self-confident through knowledge.

**All in all, that's an ongoing struggle, not just in Indonesia but, in fact, all over the world.**

You know, to be a Muslim is to be a *khalifah*,[64] a moral agent. That means that everyone is responsible for continuing the Prophetic task. The Prophetic task of human kind didn't end with Muhammad. It's the duty of every Muslim to continue *al-amr bi 'l-ma'ruf wa 'n-nahy 'an al-munkar*. Literally, this means 'enjoining what is good and forbidding what is wrong'. I conceive it as 'efforts of transformation'. We have to transform ourselves, our families and societies. That's not easy. But we have to do this prophetic task in our own capacity, as a teacher, a husband, a wife, a scholar, a brother, a sister, a politician or whatever your status and situation might be. And, like I often say, our mission will only end on judgment day. *(Musdah laughs.)*

---

[64] The concept of khalifah is, of course, related to the concept of the caliphs, the successors of the Prophet and leaders of Muslim caliphates. Yet, as a spiritual term, khalifah implies the 'stewardship' of every human being. It, thus, refers to the manner in which everyone is called by God to take care of creation and humanity. To retain the distinction between the socio-political and spiritual use of the word, different transliterations, i.e. 'caliph' and 'khalifah', respectively, were used.

# SHAHADA

In the chapter on iman, the shahada, the Islamic 'act of faith', was already mentioned as the first of the five pillars of Islam – the others being fasting, praying, giving alms and the pilgrimage to Mecca. Yet, to become a Muslim, expressing the first pillar suffices, which means one has to sincerely say the fluent sentence *"La ilaha ila Allah, Muhammadun rasulu Allah."*

This one core sentence of Islam literally translates as: "There is no god but God and Muhammad is a prophet of God." But, no matter how short and self-evident, the shahada is often misinterpreted.

A first misunderstanding would be to think that Muslims believe in a particular God, called Allah, and deny the existence of all other gods, like the God of Judaism and Christianity. This certainly isn't the case. Muslims most certainly believe in the same God for in Arabic 'al' means 'the' and 'ilah' means God. Together, they form 'Allah' or 'The God'.

The expression, "There is no other God but The God", also doesn't imply that all other Gods are 'false', but rather, it expresses that nothing else should be made into a God because God will always be greater. It is, thus, connected to the concept of tawhid as Musdah Mulia explained it. Neither power nor money nor status should ever become our Gods. We shouldn't 'worship' political leaders, wealth or material advancements. And, above all, we shouldn't make Gods of ourselves by giving in to greed or self-centredness and, thus, start to think that we can dictate others or destroy our surroundings.

Another misconception that might arise after hearing the shahada is the idea that Muhammad is the only prophet of God. This is not the case. Muhammad is simply seen as 'a' prophet, just like many other prophets before him, such as Noah, Moses or Jonah — though Muslims do, of course, see him as the 'seal' of the prophets. That is to say, they consider him to be the last prophet.

All in all, then, the Islamic tradition does not see itself as an opposition or a 'split' from the Abrahamic traditions, but rather as the continuation.

This, of course, creates a huge dilemma for Christianity, though it is seldom recognized or discussed. Yet, even those who look very sympathetically upon Islam and those who are very open to interreligious dialogue, eventually have to wonder how far they can respect the beliefs that follow from the shahada.

The first sentence of the shahada is, of course, of little concern because, in spite of what most Muslims might think, even trinity is not really a denial of the unity of the divine and Christians can easily admit to the idea that there is no god but God.

But what about Muhammad's status? What does he mean to Christians? Was he a real prophet or not?

If a Christian truly respects Islam and, indeed, accepts that Muhammad's prophecy is genuine, he also accepts the genuineness of what was revealed to him. That is to say, it means that one has to accept the Qur'an as a continuation of the Abrahamic faith. But if one does so, why would one remain a Christian?

However, if a Christian says that Muhammad wasn't a real prophet and that the Qur'an wasn't a genuine revelation, it might easily imply that Muhammad was a charlatan and a fake. Yet, such a stance obviously lacks the proper (Christian) respect.

Having journeyed as far as I have into the world of Islam — both physically and spiritually — I have come to a strange point where I can honestly express the shahada and still remain a Christian. So, yes, I do believe there is no god except *The* God. And, yes, I do believe Muhammad was a genuine prophet. But I do not become a Muslim.

How can this be so?

It's actually quite simple. I don't feel the need to convert because, in the end, I still feel more 'at home' in the Christian tradition. No matter how inspiring I might find the Qur'an and no matter how much wisdom I can learn from Muhammad's acts and words, the Gospels remain my very final source of reference and Christ remains my foremost guiding example.

If there is no god but God, then religion shouldn't be a God either. Religion is but a vehicle to remind us about God's signs. It should never be an obligation, for as the Qur'an says: "there is no compulsion in religion." When faith becomes compulsory, it loses every meaning. So wherever religions force themselves upon people, they actually annul themselves.

———— ❁ ————

Contrary to what many people might think, faith is not just a mental acceptance of certain ideas but, above all, it's a movement of the soul. Faith, in essence, is not something that forces certain concepts on people. First and foremost, faith creates an openness in the soul that enables us to witness and experience God's presence.

We can look at revelation in a very similar manner. Whether we talk about the Qur'an or Christ, revelation is more Poetry than it is Truth. You do not have to 'agree' with a poem; you have to relate to it. It's not about winning an argument; it's about seeing the beauty.

The search for that beauty became the subcutaneous theme of my conversation with the modern poet, Amir Sulaiman.

*Photo by Redouan Tijani*

# AMIR SULAIMAN
## ON THE POETRY OF CREATION

*Poetry has an important place in the history of Islam. Not only can we refer to great poets like Rumi, Attar, Hafez or Buleh Shah, but even traditional textbooks that dealt with topics like fasting, prayer or jurisprudence would often include poetry. Yet, however widespread it used to be, in recent years, it doesn't seem to have attained the same status as calligraphy or architecture. In some specific countries, such as Somalia, new generations of poets have stood up but, in general, and specifically in the West, Islamic poetry doesn't seem to flourish.*

*Someone like Amir Sulaiman is an exception, and a very solid exception for that matter. Amir is an accomplished poet, activist, recording artist and a two time HBO Def Poet. He began writing poetry at the age of twelve, and by now, his widely acclaimed slam poetry, which oozes his rap roots, has brought him to perform all over the world.*

*When I saw one of his performances for the first time, I was thoroughly impressed. His voice is strong, his spirituality deep and his performance intense. I sat down with him to talk about the importance of words, the poetry of creation and the sneaky Sméagol in all of us.*

---- ❖ ----

**Considering the importance of words in Islam because of the central place of the Qur'an as the revelation, one could expect to find 'artists of the word' wherever Islam can be found. How come there aren't more Islamic poets who are born and raised in the West?**

When Islam engages in a certain culture, it takes some time before the language is able to support the spiritual concepts. It may take a generation or two before people are able to express in their own language what Islam has brought to them. The Western Islam is still a baby nation. I'm sure that we'll see more poetry as it develops into maturity.

**Your poetry has a lot of hip hop and slam poetry influences. Do you also relate to the traditional poetry of the great icons of Islamic poetry?**

Definitely. They're a profound influence and their writing boggles my mind. Take Rumi and his *Masnavi*, for example, to write that much is one thing, but to write that much *and* make every verse a whole world in itself is simply incredible. However, when I was young, I didn't know there was such a rich tradition. I got introduced to those poets when I was already in my twenties. But nowadays, I read more of that than contemporary stuff.

The language of the Qur'an, however, has always been a strong influence on me. When I was ten years old, it gripped me because it felt so lofty and majestic, but at the same time, I was listening to hip hop, which uses street language. So, my art form is a marriage of the very lofty and the very street. It wasn't like I found Islam at a certain point and that it gradually influenced my poetry. It has always been one and the same. Islam was my faith and poetry was my personal means of expressing it. My poems also became more profound when I deepened my Islam. The centre of both is that I'm seeking to know God. Poetry is just a means to help me on that path.

## In what measure, then, do you see the Qur'an as a book of poetry?

There's a hadith that, after the death of the Prophet, someone asked his wife Aisha about his character. She described him as a 'walking Qur'an'. For me then, the Qur'an is the sitting Muhammad and Muhammad is the walking Qur'an. Also, there is something about the symmetry and mathematics of the Qur'an beyond its surface beauty, which makes you realize that it couldn't have merely come out of human inspiration. So, I don't think of it as poetry. It's a lot more.

On the other hand, I can sometimes see the whole of creation as one big poem. It's interesting to realize, for example, that the beginning of creation is seen as a verbal act. In your Christian tradition, it's in words like, "Let there be light!" And the Qur'an recounts that God said "Be" and it was. The revelation could have said God built the universe with His hands or that He poured the universe into shape, but no, he 'spoke' the universe into existence. And in the English language, the word 'universe' perfectly accords to this because it consists of 'uni', which means 'one', and 'verse', which means 'poem'. So, to me, all of creation is just one divine expression.

There is also a hadith which states that Muhammad said that the pen was the first thing created. Another hadith mentions that the intellect was the first thing created. But those two accounts don't conflict since they describe the same reality. It's all about the words. There's something very powerful in there. There was the spiritual reality and the material reality and the bridge between them is language. The mechanism that God created to bring things from non-existence into existence is the word.

## However, we aren't God and, as such, what we say isn't

**always what we bring into existence. I mean to say that our words and actions aren't always coherent because it is often difficult to practice what we preach. I'm sure that as a poet you have thought about this dilemma a great deal.**

I teach a poetry workshop and the very first thing I always mention is sincerity. It's the prerequisite for good poetry. And sincerity means two things: to *know* yourself and to *be* yourself. Reconciling what we believe and what we do is the basic question of our life. It's what we're here for. That's why rituals are important. Sometimes when people go deeper into spirituality, they start to look down upon rituals as mundane, archaic and backwards, but the reason why religions have them is exactly to keep the coherence between your acts and your words. They help to reign yourself in when you drift away. Take the five prayers, for example. If we could be fully devoted and really engrain within ourselves what we're saying, one prayer would suffice. But the truth is that we believe it when we're saying it, yet our heart shakes fifteen minutes later when we get a certain email or phone call. So, the prayer sustains our faith several times during the day. The congregational prayer, every Friday, sustains it for the week. The Ramadan sustains it for the year. And the Hajj sustains it for the lifetime. All of these practices are meant to reign the heart and the mind back in and to get rid of the distractions. And all of it is to know God. Even in the straying there is knowledge of God.

This human dilemma of always trying to get back to the divine actually is the topic of my poem 'Hallelujah'. A part of it goes like this:

> My death is my birth
> my spirit is divine but my ego is Sméagol
> my precious,
> ruthless and restless
> foolish and reckless

the only way to truly live is to die.

Meet me back in the essence.

I used the metaphor of Sméagol, the little white creature of the *Lord of the Rings*, because he's just a perfect example of raw ego. He's a fearful, manipulative, greedy and maniacal little creature – he's all of it simply because he can't let go of that one thing – that power, that 'precious'. And we're all the same. We all have this one thing that we really can't let go of and it hinders us to truly reconcile our belief and our actions.

**You say the hajj is one of the rituals that has the power to reign us back in. The poems you collected in your trilogy, 'The Meccan openings', 'The Medinan openings' and 'The openings', are also meant as a sort of 'thank you project' because your hajj was unexpectedly provided for by someone else. Did the hajj bring a fundamental change in your life?**

It did. It was a profound change and it certainly deepened my spirituality. What struck me most was the possibility to see the whole world gathering at the same place, like a mini-version of humanity. Not just because all the nationalities were there, but also because it brings together every type of person. It made me realize that, literally, everyone is searching for God – even those of whom you wouldn't think so at first. Even addicts, for example, seek a deeper connection. Whether we seek God or not, all of us are in need of a deeper connection. It's just that some are unclear about the correct direction and end up looking the wrong way, but they are looking for it nonetheless. This realization enlarged my capacity for compassion. In one of my poems, I wrote: "We are drawn to the light, like an addict to the pipe." Like an addict is being pulled towards his addiction, we are all being pulled towards God.

**Is there a verse in the Qur'an that 'pulls' you to God more**

**than others?**

Different verses inspire me at different times in my life, of course, but right now it's verses one to three of Surah An-Nasr: "When God's help comes and He opens up your path; when you see people coming into the way of God in huge droves, then glorify Him, praise Him and ask forgiveness for He's the one who can accept repentance." I find myself repeating this in my daily prayers. There's the literal meaning on the one hand of many people coming to Islam, but on the other hand, I interpret the 'droves' as all the beings, the states and personalities that are living inside of myself. And I pray that all of them would be coming into the way of God — even my Sméagol.

**You have said a lot about the importance and the power of words, but when you speak of the effort to focus the whole of our being on God, we can easily reach a point where words become insufficient.**

True. To know *about* God is not the same as to *know God*. You can know much *about* the Prophets and their teachings, *about* how God revealed himself, at what times, and so on, but to really *know Him* is something different. It's the same in human relations. You can know someone's history and character, but that's different than knowing someone through a marital bond or like a father relates to his son. There's a level of intimacy beyond words.
In the end, all the words of the saints are a bit like running in place since they try to express their experiences of God even though it's unutterable. Whatever we say about God, God is beyond it all. Even when we let our mind expand tremendously and imagine the most sublime things, God is still beyond it. But the poet can't resist; he has to try to express it nonetheless.

# IBRAHIM

Jesus, of course, didn't think of himself as a Christian. He saw himself as a Jew. Muhammad also did not see himself as a Muslim because he thought he had founded a new religion. When he used the word Muslim, he did so because he saw Muslims as those people who accepted the revelations of the Prophets and devoted themselves to God. The Prophet, therefore, used the word Muslim more as a somewhat generic term for believers or – in line with its literal translation – devotees.[65]

The previous piece on the shahada already made it clear that the first Muslim community never saw themselves and their faith as a break from the old existing traditions around them, such as Judaism and Christianity, but rather saw it as the continuation of the original monotheistic religion. In a sense, therefore, Muhammad and the first Muslims actually saw themselves as some sort of 'Abrahamists', as followers of Abraham – who's called 'Ibrahim' in Arabic.

---

[65] The words 'Islam' and 'Muslim', just like Salam, stem from the root of S-L-M, which implies 'to be whole, to be intact'. Their meaning of 'submission' or 'devotion' are closely linked to the spiritual concept of 'becoming whole' by surrendering the ego and allowing God to fill the soul.

When we read the Qur'an, we quickly come across many references to Jewish prophets. Jesus and Mary also receive a prominent place. There's even a complete surah dedicated to Mary, and it's a widely held Muslim belief that Jesus will return at the Day of Judgement to restore justice.

From the very start, therefore, Islam and Christianity actually weren't strangers but brothers. Sadly enough, throughout history, they became ever more estranged, even to the extent that the Crusades of the Middle Ages and the contemporary ideology of clashing civilisations could become the general image of the relationship between these siblings.

Through God's grace, however, there have always been people who refused to bow their heads to such conflict and tension. Instead, they tried to embrace with friendship and understanding.

In this respect, I often refer to Saint Francis. As most Christians know, Saint Francis was a mystic and ascetic monk from the thirteenth century and one of the most important reformers and saints of Christian history. During one of the Crusades, Saint Francis succeeded in having a conversation with Al Kamil, the Sultan of Egypt. What strikes me again and again in the story is the fact that a nonviolent ascetic, who walked barefoot, could cross a restless warzone and eventually reach the Sultan without a scratch. They discussed faith and religion, while neither one thought of beheading the other. The Sultan even gave Saint Francis official permission to visit the grave of Christ and to freely travel the area. Saint Francis' nonviolence, therefore, got him a lot further than the belligerence of the Crusaders.

Christians tend to forget, however, that Francis wasn't the only man of peace in this historic occurrence. Convinced that Islam is a violent religion, they mostly assume without much critical thought that the Muslims were just as aggressive as the Crusaders. This isn't true at all. Sultan Al Kamil, in fact, made many peace proposals – even at times when he greatly dominated the battles – but the leaders of the Christian armies consistently refused these offers.

Today, the same still holds true. A large number of 'peace seekers' can be found on both sides. Efforts of interreligious dialogue and interfaith projects are initiated by Muslims just as much as Christians.

The 'Common Word' initiative, which was started by Prince Ghazi bin Muhammad bin Talal of Jordan, is probably the best known international example of such a Muslim peace gesture in the last few years. It was a letter from leaders of the Islamic religion to leaders of the Christian religion written in response to Pope Benedict XVI's lecture at the University of Regensburg on 12 September 2006, which had aroused some controversy because he had made some unfavourable remarks about Islam during that lecture. The 'Common Word' letter, thus, called for peace between Muslims and Christians. It asked for strengthened efforts on both sides that might lead to a better understanding between both religions. Hundreds of prominent Muslim leaders signed the letter.

———— ✿ ————

My Halal Monk journey is, therefore, only one small and humble attempt among many works of reconciliation. And it was only a matter of time before I would meet a Muslim who had already made his or her own journey through Christianity. Hence, my conversation with Mona Siddiqui closed the circle of my journey.

Mona Siddiqui is a Professor of Islamic and Interreligious Studies at the University of Edinburgh and a regular contributor to the BBC, *The Times*, *The Scotsman*, *The Guardian* and the *Sunday Herald*. Yet, the reason I specifically wanted to talk to her was because of her research on the place of Jesus in Islam.

# MONA SIDDIQUI
## ON JESUS IN ISLAM
## AND INTERFAITH HUMBLENESS

*The highly respected Pakistani-British academic, Mona Siddiqui, focusses on two distinct fields of research. As a professor at Edinburgh University, her primary area of interest is classical Islamic law, juristic arguments and the interface with contemporary ethical issues. Her second focus, however, is the theological history of Christian-Muslim relations. Her concern for the subject grew through her involvement in a series of international seminars convened by the former archbishop of Canterbury, Rowan Williams. But it became more than just some side-line interest. She's the patron, for example, of The Feast, a youth work charity which focusses on community cohesion between Christian and Muslim teenagers. And in 2011, Siddiqui was eventually appointed Officer of the Order of the British Empire for her services to inter-faith relations.*

*In 2013, Prof. Siddiqui also wrote the interesting book, 'Christians, Muslims and Jesus' which delves deeper into the various views Muslims held of Jesus throughout history, and the ways in which these views determined the relationship between the two faiths.*

---

## What brought you to study Jesus in Islam?

Through my encounters with many Christians, I simply came to realize that Jesus was the focus of many theological questions and differences between the two faiths. So, I gradually felt the subject needed more attention.

Of course, the Qur'an has a particular theme, which is that Muhammad is walking the same path as the Old Testament prophets, such as Abraham, Moses, as well as Jesus. The Qur'an also relates that Jesus was born to a virgin called Mary, preached God's word, gathered disciples and performed miracles. Jesus will even return to Earth, according to Islamic tradition, as al-Masih – the Messiah. But the crucial difference from the Christian narrative lies in the essence of prophetic revelation, however. For Muslims, Jesus cannot be acknowledged as 'the Son of God'. Within Islam, revelation appears but divine distance is maintained, while for Christians, God is revealed in Christ and, as such, distance is overcome. And I find this theological difference in the modes of God's disclosure quite fascinating.

**This poignantly summarizes the traditional Islamic and Qur'anic view on Jesus and you point out the crucial theological aspects that make it different from the Christian view. But how would you describe the symbolic or spiritual meaning of Jesus in the lives of Muslims — if there is any at all?**

I could, of course, refer to a statement like Rumi's that Jesus is a prophet in whom the attributes of God became manifest, but eventually the Muslim community holds Muhammad in ultimate veneration. Even though Muslims revere Jesus as God's prophet and messenger, there is no understanding of Jesus as God incarnate. It's only in scholarly debates you'll find Muslims talking about Jesus from a variety of perspectives. On a daily level, people will simply say He's one of the prophets. But he has little 'devotional value'.

**So, although Jesus could be a perfect bridge figure between Christianity and Islam, because he doesn't feature in the daily life of Muslims and because, theologically speaking, He will also always be the quintessential element on which 'the twain shall never meet', there is little chance of Him becoming such a bridge figure?**

The two don't have to meet anyway. Dialogue isn't necessarily about bridging anything. It's about understanding themes, persons and ways of looking at how God expresses Himself in different religions. So, the interest in Jesus isn't to say: "Oh, now we've reached some good compromise." Certainly, for me personally, it's more about trying to understand another way of looking at God, and about wondering how I can make sense of it as a Muslim.

**That reminds me of something that happened at an interreligious dialogue group I once attended. The group read and discussed certain passages from both the Qur'an and the Bible that focussed on similar topics. Suddenly, however, the tone of the conversation became quite tense when it got to a very crucial difference between the two traditions: some of the Christians said that God was in need of humans in order to relate to them. For Muslims, of course, this is quite unthinkable. In their view, God doesn't *need* anyone. This difference isn't all that surprising since the Qur'an often emphasises the ultimate self-sufficiency of the divine, while Christianity stems from the very idea that God became human. That was one of the many moments that increasingly convinced me that efforts of interfaith dialogue shouldn't be trying too obsessively to find common ground. Perhaps more than that, they should, in fact, focus on**

**learning to accept the difference.**

It shouldn't even be about that necessarily. It's simply about exploring the fact that you noticed a fundamental difference. It might make you wonder how the God of Christians and Muslims can be one and the same if they have such different understandings of God. And it might make you dig deeper into your own tradition as well.

There are many ways of talking about God in relation to sin and repentance, mercy and compassion which open up all kinds of dialogue. There are hadiths that recount how someone went to the Prophet and asked him to give him a prayer that would prevent him from sinning ever again, yet God told him: "Don't give him such a prayer, for if my servant does not sin, upon whom will I bestow my mercy?" So, does God need us after all, if He wants us to turn to him for repentance?

I remember using such hadiths in a talk once and asking the question, "Does God want us to sin?" There were Muslims in the audience who were annoyed and thought I couldn't say such a thing. But I can say whatever I want. It's just exploring the idea. It doesn't mean I know anything more about God. It's a theological exercise to see what we can make of such texts and traditions. Constructive dialogue does not reduce one's faith, it rather enlarges it.

A Muslim could, therefore, say: God has no need. Full stop. But hearing Christians talk about the 'humanization' of God can, in many ways, also make you reassess the manner in which you think about God as a Muslim.

**But if dialogue does not have a specific goal and is only an exploration, don't we then deny its capacity to dispel certain prejudices and conflicts?**

Of course, if people are getting together in community groups to get to know each other, that's great. Because at the community level, people might have misconceptions about many things that can easily be clarified by simply talking to each other. But if you do scholarly work, you have to be open to the possibility that there might be no definitive outcome at all.

Actually, one of the pitfalls of efforts of dialogue is the idea that we should reach some kind of goal with which we should all be happy. I'm opposed to a 'dialogue on the surface' as well. We need to go deeper. But how do you know you've gone deep enough? It makes no sense to say: "Oh, this is deep enough." It's just about trying to understand how people talk about the things that matter to us in life. And once you start to look at it like that, you don't go into any dialogue setting with some sort of intended goal. You're just there to learn. You're not there to defend your viewpoint, but to listen to how somebody else is expressing themes that you're interested in as well.

**Which implies you learned a lot through your own interaction with the Christian theological tradition.**

Absolutely. And we actually touched on it already: there is a vulnerability in talking about God that Christians have and that Muslims don't. Muslims are very certain about God. Christians might be very certain about their convictions, but the way they talk about God and His vulnerability is not something that we have in our vocabulary. And that's quite intriguing. It makes me wonder, most of our convictions about God, are they convictions because that's really what we believe or are they convictions because that's what we derive out of centuries of theological thinking? I already mentioned some hadiths, but I could just as well refer to someone like Ibn Arabi who said that God created creation so that creation would love Him. There is vulnerability there. But, on the whole, these questions weren't the central questions asked by Muslim theologians because they were concerned more with human worship, adoration and love for God as opposed to God's love for us.

**It's interesting you mention this 'vulnerability' as something you've learned. During my own journey through Islam, the 'certainty' of Muslims and the way they put God so strongly at the forefront have been some sort of 'mirror' for me. Even something as basic as the fact that many Muslims pray five times a day continuously challenges me.**

A good friend of mine, who's an American scholar, spent a long time in Jerusalem and has recently gone back to the States. When he gives lectures – often for a Christian public – he sometimes says: "When I hear the adhan, the call to prayer, it always touches me. I've been listening to it five times a day for years in a row, but I'm still so moved by the 'come to prayer, come to prayer' and when it resounds, I feel like I want to go and pray with the Muslims. But then I stop because in so many inscriptions in mosques it reads: 'He didn't begat neither was he begotten.'[66] And that stops me in my tracks because I realize they still deny what is fundamental to my belief."
I think that's quite beautiful. He's not saying he rejects anything, but he's saying that there is always a certain call in somebody's faith and it has a way of inviting all of us to look for God. We may not, in the end, respond to it the way a believer would, but the very fact that we're pulled in that direction is really quite moving.

**When we speak of encounters with other religions, 'being moved', indeed, seems far more important than being convinced.**

---

[66] A Qur'anic sentence that often places itself within the theological discussion about the nature of Christ and the question of whether or not He is the son of God.

When we are looking for a bridge, we have to realize that there's emotional and intellectual common ground. And often, the intellectual common ground turns out to be of little importance in the lived lives of people. In the lived lives, it's mostly the sense of love for God that moves Christians and the sense of compassion of God that moves Muslims. There's a lot more common ground there.

**Which is why, in some of your writings, you have made a plea for a theology of compassion, rather than a theology of salvation, is it not?**

Indeed. It has changed a little, but I think that for too long, traditional interreligious dialogue was about whether someone would be 'saved'. But how do we talk about people in terms of salvation? You get nowhere with that. In strict Muslim theology, I don't even know whether I'll be saved myself – whatever that may be – so how am I making pronouncements about anyone else? In a way, therefore, that's almost a futile exercise for me. I would never stand up and say: "Jews and Christians can't be saved because the Qur'an has an ambivalent relationship with them." The truth is that I don't know what the truth is. But there's that sense . . . that sense that God is always present in our own nature as human beings. And that sense makes it possible to relate to one another. So, *being* in a certain way, just being humble for example, is a theological exercise as well — and a very important one for that matter.

# A FINAL
# REFLECTION

When I asked Abdal Hakim Murad where the real centres of authority are found, his unexpected answer was to look beyond the worldly powers and toward the living saints. "Their self is gone", he said, "and only the Prophetic form remains. The dignity, the ancient wisdom, the selflessness, the love for others . . . you see it in the Prophet and you see it in the saint."

In the end, Shaykh Murad's answer turns out to be exemplary of a theme all my encounters have in common. Almost all the people I was graced to meet emphasised the importance of looking beyond literalism – both the literalism of the religious extremists, as well as the literalism of the staunch materialists. They oppose an excessive consumer society, but just as well, they denounce religious rigidity. They root themselves strongly in Islamic tradition, but they do not limit their religion to a set of convictions, rules and physical appearances.

As such, many of them show a way out of aggression and conflict not only through words, but above all through example. Not their specific beliefs, but their gentle characters, their sense of justice and their compassionate hearts were proof of their Islam.

Their examples can, therefore, thoroughly shake the tree of our 'Christian subconscious'. And when we allow that subconscious to be shaken, we will notice how it has a tendency to excessively emphasise faith and conviction as the core aspects of religion. On top of this, since many of the Western values, norms and ethics are derived from the Christian culture and subconscious, we will notice that the Western world, in general, is too focused on 'correct convictions'.

That's exactly why we debate how compatible Islam is or isn't with democracy, or why religious convictions, in general, are often evaluated by asking how much they accept or reject certain scientific findings.

However, I hope the conversations in this book have shown that dichotomies, such as democracy vs. Islam, science vs. religion or modern freedom vs. suppressive tradition, make little sense. Furthermore, I hope they clarified that we will only make it worse if we continue to impose such dichotomies on the present day debates.

If we truly want to rid ourselves of contemporary tensions, we will first need to realise that religion isn't about being 'right', but about being 'good'. So, we shouldn't look at the current conflicts between the West and the Islamic world as a problem of clashing ideas or incompatible cultures. They aren't arguments that can be won by someone who's right. They can only be overcome when all of us try to be humble.

It makes no sense, therefore, to ask Muslims to be more moderate Muslims. In fact, we should support Muslims to be better Muslims, just like we should support Jews to be better Jews and Christians to be better Christians. Compassion, justice and humanity aren't the result of moderate convictions. They're the result of a deepened soul.

———— ❀ ————

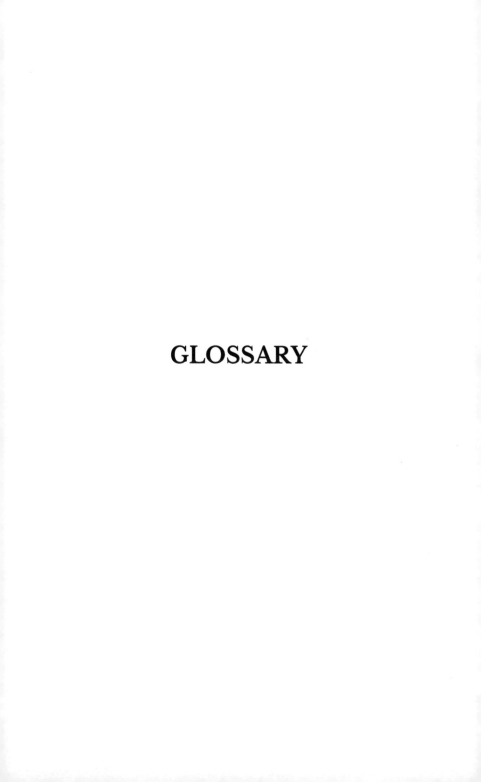

# GLOSSARY

Adhan | The Islamic call to prayer. In Muslim countries. it can be heard five times a day as it resounds from the rooftops of the mosques.

Ahl al-Kitab | Literally: people of the book. The term designates non-Muslim adherents to faiths which have a revealed scripture. The Qur'an mentions Jews, Sabians and Christians as three types of adherents, though it does not say these are the only ones. The concept of 'people of the book' should, therefore, not by definition be limited to these three.

Al-Andalus | Also known as 'Muslim Spain' or 'Islamic Iberia'. It does not coincide with the contemporary Andalusia but refers to a medieval cultural domain and territory under Muslim rule, occupying at its peak most of contemporary Spain and Portugal.

Al-Azhar | An important Egyptian University in Cairo. It was founded around 970 AD and is, therefore, one of the very first universities in the world. Still today, it is one of the most important academic strongholds in the Muslim world.

Al-Fatiha | The opening chapter of the Qur'an. It reads: "In the name of God, the Lord of Mercy, the Giver of Mercy! Praise belongs to God, Lord of the Worlds, the Lord of Mercy, the Giver of Mercy, Master of the Day of Judgement. It is You we worship; it is You we ask for help. Guide us to the straight path: the path of those You have blessed, those who incur no anger and who have not gone astray." (M.A.S. Abdel Haleem, The Qur'an. A new translation, Oxford University Press, 2004.)

Arkan al-Islam | See 'five pillars of Islam'.

Burqa | A long, loose garment covering the whole body from head to foot.

Caliph | Literally 'successor' or 'caretaker'. The term refers to a successor of the Prophet and, thus, to a leader of a Muslim community. A caliph ruled in Baghdad until 1258 and then in Egypt until the Ottoman conquest of 1517; the title was then held by the Ottoman sultans until their lineage was broken by the formation of the Turkish republic. Apart from its socio-political meaning, the word caliph or khalifah also carries the spiritual meaning of 'stewardship' over creation and humanity. See Khalifah for this disambiguation.

Caliphate    An Islamic sovereign polity led by a caliph. The different Muslim empires that have succeeded one another are, therefore, usually described as caliphates. The Ottoman Empire was the last caliphate and was abolished by Atatürk in 1924. The caliphate that was proclaimed by Abu Bakr al-Baghdadi in 2014 wasn't recognized by the great majority of Muslims and, as such, cannot be properly considered a real caliphate.

Dar al-Islam    Literally translated it means 'the House of Islam'. It is a term used to refer to the 'world of Islam' or, put differently, those areas in the world where Islam is practiced.

Dhikr    An Islamic devotional act and method of prayer. It displays many similarities to the repetition of mantras. It typically involves the recitation of the Names of God and/or supplications taken from hadith or Qur'anic verses. The word 'dhikr' can literally be translated as 'remembrance' and it is a shortened form of 'dhikr ullah'. The practice is, therefore, seen as a way of 'remembering' and 'reminding' God.

Fana    A term the mystics used to describe the spiritual point where the ego is finally removed and unity with the divine is reached. It can be translated as 'passing away', 'annihilation' or 'evaporation'.

Fatwa    A juridical/theological 'advice' or 'opinion' of a certain scholar. When scholars are confronted with a question about the correct conduct in certain situations, they formulate their stance on the matter and base this stance on their interpretation of sharia, hadith and Qur'an. This stance and the argumentation leading up to it is a fatwa. Traditionally, fatwas were, therefore, only presented after thorough debate between different scholars and after solid research of the scriptural sources. One scholar's fatwa can, thus, also easily deny the fatwa of another.

Fiqh

Fiqh is Islamic jurisprudence. Literally, the word fiqh is translated as 'understanding' and, as such, refers to the effort of trying to understand the sharia. In other words, fiqh is the 'practice' that seeks to unravel the divine law of the sharia and that searches for the practical expressions of the sharia within daily life.

Five pillars of Islam

It is commonly accepted that there are five pillars upon which the Islamic faith is built. The first and most important pillar is the shahada, the creed of faith. The others pillars are sawm (fasting during the month of Ramadan), salat (praying, preferably five times a day), zakat (giving alms) and the hajj (pilgrimage to Mecca).

Hadith

A report of the sayings and acts of the Prophet.

Hajj

The pilgrimage to Mecca, which Muslims are supposed to perform at least once in their lifetime if physically and financially able. It is one of the five pillars of Islam.

Halal

What is proper or lawful. Most people know the term halal in relation to food, for example, because of the fact that animals have to be slaughtered in a ritual way before they can be deemed to be halal. But halal and its counterpart, haram, can be applied to almost any act or product. When the fiqh has determined that certain deeds or the use of certain products are in accordance with the sharia, they are considered to be proper and lawful and, thus, halal. And when, on the other hand, the fiqh has determined that certain deeds or the use of certain products transgress the sharia, scholars will deem them haram and Muslims should, therefore, refrain from them.

Haram    What is improper or forbidden. It stands in opposition to halal.

Hijab    The common headscarf, which covers the hair.

Ihsan    Often referred to as the last of the three dimensions of the Islamic religion. The other two are Islam ('spiritual submission' as it is expressed in the five pillars) and iman (the six aspects of faith). Ihsan combines the other two. That is to say, ihsan is the coherence between one's faith and one's actions.

Ijtihad    The process of personal and independent theological and spiritual interpretation. A more elaborate explanation can be found on p. 187 and onwards.

Iman    Often translated as 'belief'. It refers to the acceptance of certain metaphysical premises of the Muslim faith. It's mostly summarized in six articles: belief in God, belief in the angels, belief in divine books, belief in the prophets, belief in the Day of Judgment and belief in God's predestination.

Jihad    It is often thought that the term 'jihad' refers to some sort of obligatory 'holy war' that Muslims have to wage to impose Islamic rule all over the world. But jihad, in fact, simply means 'striving'. As such, it could indeed refer to an 'armed striving' to win a defensive battle, but it can just as well refer to the inner striving of a believer to become a better human being. A more elaborate explanation can be found on p. 175 and onwards.

Jihadi    Someone pursuing jihad. Today, it has become a term that specifically means a militant Muslim.

Jinn    A supernatural being from Islamic mythology and theology. It's a sort of invisible spirit that can also

| | |
|---|---|
| | take hold of human beings. The English word 'genie' is derived from this Arabic word. |
| Khadi | A Muslim judge. |
| Khalifah | In a 'social' or 'political' sense, the concept of khalifah refers to the successors of the Prophet and leaders of Muslim caliphates. This concurs with the English word 'caliph'. In a spiritual sense, however, khalifah implies the 'stewardship' of every human being. It, thus, refers to the manner in which everyone is called by God to take care of creation and humanity. To retain the distinction between these two senses, different transliterations were used. |
| Maqam | A melodic phrase of a set of notes that are connected through traditional musical relationships and patterns. |
| Maqasid al Sharia | The 'intentions' of the Sharia. That is to say, they are the underlying purpose behind the Islamic laws. |
| Masnavi | Rumi's most important work. It's an educational mystical poem. It's discussed more deeply in the conversation with Abdulwahid Van Bommel. See p. 153 and onwards. |
| Mecelle | The civil code of the Ottoman Empire in the late 19th and early 20th centuries. It was the first attempt to codify a part of the Sharia-based law of an Islamic state. |
| Mi'raj | Literally it means 'ladder'. It refers to the spiritual ascension of Muhammad during one particular night. The Islamic tradition relates a story of the Prophet ascending on the heavenly steed, Buraq, to the seven circles of Heaven where he speaks with earlier prophets such as Abraham (Ibrahim), Moses (Musa), John the Baptist (Yahya) and Jesus (Isa). |
| Millet system | In the Ottoman Empire, a millet was a specific confessional community, recognized by the |

Ottoman rulers. These millets were allowed to decide on much of their internal affairs according to their own religious laws and regulations – Muslim according to the Sharia law, Christians according to their Canon law and Jews according to the Halakha.

Mufti
An Islamic scholar who is an interpreter of sharia and, thus, an expounder of fiqh.

Mujahid
Someone who's 'involved' in jihad; that is to say, someone who struggles on the path of Allah.

Mutasawwif
Someone who adheres to a mystical school or who places him/herself within a mystical tradition.

Naqshbandi
A Sufi tariqa that originated in the twelfth century out of the teachings of Yusuf Hamdani and Abdul Khaliq Gajadwani. The latter is regarded as the shaykh who introduced the silent dhikr, one of the practices which is typical of the Naqshbandi. Whereas dhikr will be performed out loud in many tariqas, the Naqshbandi remain quiet when repeating their specific devotional phrases.

Nawazil fiqh
Jurisprudence of momentous events. At certain times and in certain places, the 'normal' theological and juridical implications of fiqh might not apply because of particular problems or emergency situations. In such instances, new rulings have to be sought that allow Muslims to adapt to the unforeseen circumstances and still remain in accordance with the sharia.

Ney
A reed flute which produces a very soft mellow tone. It's the most important instrument of Ottoman Sufi music.

Niqab
A veil that covers everything except the eyes.

Pancasila
The official philosophical foundation of the Indonesian state. Pancasila consists of two old Javanese words (originally from Sanskrit), 'panca' meaning 'five', and 'sila' meaning 'principles'. These

five principles include spirituality, humanity, unity of the country, democracy, and social justice.

**Panjtan Pak**

An Urdu word that combines Prophet Mohammad, Ali (the Prophet's nephew and son-in-law), Fatimah (the wife of Ali and daughter of the Prophet), Hassan (the first son of Ali and Fatimah) and Hussain (the second son of Ali and Fatimah).

**Qawwali**

A type of devotional music from Pakistan. The tradition recounts that it was invented by Amir Khusrow to spread the message of Islam in a musical way. Qawwali songs (or rather, recitations) are always based on the poems of the mystics and saints. They are performed in a group, mostly of nine to twelve people, consisting of a lead singer with backing vocals, supported by tabla, harmonium and clapping.

**Quraysh**

A powerful merchant tribe that controlled Mecca (and consequently also the access to the Ka'aba) at the time of the Prophet. Muhammad was born into the Banu Hashim clan of the Quraysh tribe. Because the leaders of the Quraysh did not accept his prophethood, conflicts arose and Muhammad had to flee to Medina. Only when the Quraysh were finally defeated could the Muslim community return to Mecca.

**Rumi**

A poet, mystic and saint from the thirteenth century who was of enormous influence on the literature, spirituality and theology of the whole Islamic world. He is commonly known as Mevlana Rumi, though his original name was Jelal Al Din Muhammad Balkhi. He received the name 'Rumi' because the word 'Rum' was derived from the word 'Roman' and designated the Byzantine region on the border of the Muslim world. The word 'mevlana', on the other hand, comes from Persian and means 'master' or 'teacher'. So, the way we know Rumi nowadays is actually as 'the spiritual master of the Byzantine region'.

Salafi            An adherent of Salafism.

Salafism          A particular movement within Islam that strictly
                  focusses on the first sources of Islam. Therefore, its
                  practices are based solely on the Qur'an and the
                  example of the Prophet and his companions. In
                  fact, the term 'salafi' takes its name from the word
                  salaf, which means 'predecessors' or 'ancestors' and
                  is used to identify the earliest Muslims. Thus, Salafis
                  try to conform as much as possible to the life of
                  those earliest Muslims. Yet, in itself, the Salafi
                  movement is a very modern reactionary movement
                  that denounces many other aspects of the Islamic
                  tradition that were built up during the centuries
                  because they see them as unlawful innovations.

Sema              The traditional ritual of the Mevlevi Order of Jelal
                  Al Din Rumi. Wearing long white robes and a
                  brown fez on their heads, those partaking in the
                  ritual will whirl around their axis in a meditative
                  effort to come closer to the divine. It's what gave
                  the nickname 'whirling dervishes' to the adherents
                  of the order.

Shahada           The Muslim 'creed of faith'. It is the first of the five
                  pillars of Islam. To become a Muslim, it suffices to
                  genuinely express this shahada: "La ilaha ila Allah,
                  Muhammadun rasulu Allah." This one core
                  sentence of Islam literally translates as: "There is no
                  god but God and Muhammad is a prophet of God."

Sharia            The ordinances of God. Contrary to what many
                  people think, the sharia is not set out in explicit
                  legal codes nor is it written down clearly in the
                  Qur'an or some other book. As a concept, it refers
                  to the moral implications of the divine law that
                  undergirds life. Throughout history however, the
                  exact nature and content of the sharia has remained
                  a never ending matter of interpretation and debate.
                  Just like our present day juridical systems, the
                  Islamic 'juridotheology' of sharia and fiqh has
                  always been discussed and re-discussed among

different scholars, factions, orders and schools. The concept is more elaborately dealt with on p. 79 and onwards.

| | |
|---|---|
| Shaykh | An honorific that literally means 'elder' and which is given to someone who's the leader of a community. As such, it might refer to the leader of a tribe or clan in a political sense, but in a religious sense, it will refer to the spiritual leader or teacher of a particular religious community. In traditional spiritual settings, it is often the case that students of a particular shaykh are granted the honorific by the shaykh himself once they are ready to teach others. |
| Shia | One of the main denominations of Muslims. About 10 to 15 per cent of Muslims are Shia. Shia Muslims can be predominantly found in Iran and Iraq, and within large minority communities in Afghanistan, Pakistan, Yemen, Bahrain, Syria, and Lebanon. For the difference between Shia and Sunni see 'Sunni-Shia conflict'. |
| Shirk | Creating an idol and worshipping something or someone other than God. |
| Sufi | A mystic. The word Sufi is, today, commonly used to designate 'an adherent of Sufism'. Yet as Dr. D. Latifa explains (see p. 119 and the following), the word Sufi was always traditionally used to describe the (mystical) saints. Contrary to its contemporary usage, therefore, the word Sufi was not used to express someone's belonging to a particular group or branch of Islam. Rather, it was a title that expressed respect for people who were seen as spiritually highly evolved. The Sufi is, therefore, someone who has reached the end of the mystical path, while someone who is still trying to walk the mystical path is called a mutasawwif. In English, however, the word Sufi is commonly used for both a Sufi and a mutasawwif. |
| Sufiana Kalam | A type of devotional music from Pakistan. As with qawwali music, the songs (or rather, recitations) are |

based on the poems of the mystics and saints. In Sufiana Kalam, however, they are performed by one particular singer, backed up by just one or a couple of musicians.

Sufis

The English plural of Sufi. In this book, the word is used in its common meaning as those who adhere to a mystical school or who place themselves within a mystical tradition. In Arabic, they would be called mutasawwifa.

Sufism

Islamic mysticism. It is a broad denominator for an enormous variety of spiritual and mystical teachings, practices and traditions. In my conversations with Peter Sanders, Abdal Hakim Murad, Abdulwahid Van Bommel, Kudsi Ergüner and Dr. D. Latifa, I go much deeper into this aspect of the Islamic tradition and the misconceptions surrounding it.

Sufiya

The Arabic plural of Sufi. In this book, the word is used to refer to the highly respected mystical saints of the Islamic tradition in order to distinguish from the word 'sufis', which might also imply mutasawwif.

Sunnah

The 'lifestyle' of the Muslim. Literally, it means 'tradition'. It is the Islamic way of life prescribed as normative on the basis of the Prophet's example in the way he spoke, acted and behaved.

Sunni

One of the main denominations of Muslims. About 85 to 90 per cent of Muslims are Sunni. For the difference between Sunni and Shia see 'Sunni-Shia conflict'.

Sunni-Shia conflict

The original split between Sunni and Shia was mainly a disagreement about the succession of the leadership of the early Muslim community. After the death of the Prophet, he was succeeded by the four rightly guided caliphs (Abu Bakr, Umar, Uthman ibn Affan and Ali). When Ali, the nephew and son-in-law of the Prophet became caliph, certain groups revolted against him. Those who supported Ali and who thought that the following caliphs should belong to Ali's lineage became the Shia. After Ali was murdered, however, Muawiyah became the next caliph and those who kept on following the caliph became the Sunni. Throughout the centuries, certain doctrinal and ritual differences have arisen, such as the emphasis on reverence for Ali in Shia Islam or the division in different 'schools of law' in Sunni Islam. Conflicts between (subgroups of) Sunni and Shia would often surface, but, in spite of what many people think, Sunni and Shia have most often lived peacefully together, as exemplified by the fact that both Sunni and Shia have always come together for the hajj in Mecca. Because of the geo-politics of the last decades, however, the division has often been rekindled and strengthened to serve other purposes. This can, for example, be seen in the Iran-Iraq war of the 1980s, in the doctrinal radicalisation of the Taliban during the 1990s and in the insurgences in Syria and Iraq in the 2010s.

Surah    A chapter in the Qur'an.

Tafsir    The explanatory interpretations of Qur'anic verses.

Taqwa    Mostly translated as 'the fear of God'. A somewhat broader interpretation is 'god-consciousness'. In Muslim theology, taqwa is, therefore, a concept that refers to a constant awareness of Allah's presence and a remembrance of a Muslim's relationship and responsibility to Allah as his creation and servant.

Tariqa    A school, brotherhood or order.

Tasawwuf    The inner, spiritual and mystical dimension of Islam.

Tawhid    The (doctrine of the) unity of God. It is one of the core concepts of Islamic monotheism. It's the belief that there is only one God and that this God is not divided within himself. Everything flows from Him and everything returns to Him, but even though he can be witnessed, perceived and even experienced within all of creation, his unique transcendence ultimately remains untouched by the coming and passing of all that exists.

Ulama

The group of Muslims who have been educated in several aspects of Islamic theology and jurisprudence and, thus, have the credentials and authority to explain religion and its implications to other people and to discuss it among other scholars.

Ummah

Nation or community. It is distinguished from Sha'b which means a nation with common ancestry or geography. As such, Ummah refers to community that is not bound by lineage or place and has, by now, become synonymous with the worldwide Muslim community.

Wahdat al-wujud

One of the two differing views on the ontology of the unity of the soul within Islamic mysticism. The idea of wahdat al-wujud, which literally means 'unity of existence', maintains that total unification with the divine is possible. This is in contrast to the wahdat ash-shuhud.

Wahdat ash-shuhud

One of the two differing views on the ontology of the unity of the soul within Islamic mysticism. The idea of wahdat ash-shuhud, which literally means 'unity of perception', maintains that one can eventually only be a 'witness' of the divine. As such, there remains a distinction between oneself and God, and one's connection to God is somewhat more 'from the outside'. This is in contrast to the wahdat al-wujud.

Wahhabism

A particular form of Salafism which became the official ideology of the Saudi State. It is based on the teachings of Muhammad Ibn Abdal Wahhab. Wahhabis do not like the term 'Wahhabism', and prefer Salafis or Muwahhidun, the latter meaning 'unitarians'.

# About the author

Jonas Yunus Atlas is a scholar and activist from Belgium. He writes and lectures on religion, mysticism and societal change. Spiritually, he's rooted within the Christian tradition, although, for many years, he also immersed himself into various Eastern religions.  After his studies in philosophy, anthropology and theology at different universities he became active in all sorts of local and international peace work. His texts, essays and books can be found at *www.jonasyunus.net*.

The revised edition of his book, *Breath: The inner essence of meditation and prayer*, was published in January 2015. This little gem beautifully elucidates the flow of our mind, heart and soul during meditation and prayer. It explains how we can guide our inner being to moments of spiritual contemplation. In a concise and poetic language, Jonas Yunus Atlas clarifies the core aspects of meditation and prayer. He does not discuss their outer forms or technical aspects, but reveals their mental forms and deeper spirit. And, while doing so, he reframes our relationship with the divine. Many meditation books focus on bodily exercises and physical postures that are needed to open distinct energy channels. The verses in this book, however, describe the different 'spiritual postures' that open the 'channels of the soul' between ourselves and God.

# About Yunus Publishing

Yunus Publishing produces inspirational web and print projects. It mainly publishes the texts and books of Jonas Yunus Atlas (both in English and Dutch), but also maintains his Halal Monk website and projects such as the thoughtsofgandhi.org, a web tool that allows people to receive weekly Gandhi quotes through a newsletter or various social media.

### To be informed of future releases
If you would like to be informed of new publications and web projects of Yunus Publishing, please subscribe to the newsletter on *yunuspublishing.org*. You will only be contacted when a new book or web project is launched; your address will never be shared and you can unsubscribe at any time.

### A kind request
Word-of-mouth is, of course, crucial for any type of publication or inspirational project. So, if you enjoyed this book, please consider leaving a review at Amazon.com or the retailer where you purchased it. Even if it's only a line or two, it can be a huge help for a small publishing endeavour such as ours.

### Contact
For any comments, questions or requests, you're always welcome to send an e-mail to: *mail@yunuspublishing.org*.

*www.jonasyunus.net*
*www.yunuspublishing.org*

CPSIA information can be obtained
at www.ICGtesting.com
Printed in the USA
LVHW021935231221
707057LV00002B/207

9 789081 499644